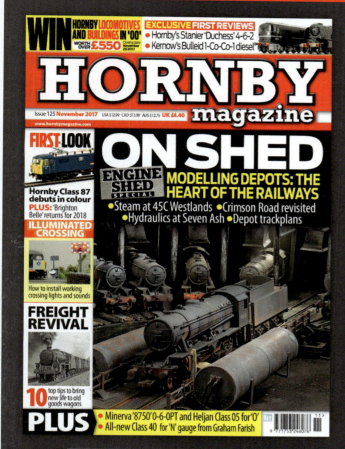

What's inside...

EDITORIAL
Editor: Mike Wild
Assistant Editor: Mark Chivers
Sub Editor: Andy Roden
Contributors: Evan Green-Hughes, Tim Shackleton, Paul Chetter, Ben Jones, Julia Scarlett and Ian Wild.
Senior designer: Steve Diggle

REGISTERED OFFICE
Units 1-4, Gwash Way Industrial Estate, Ryhall Road, Stamford, Lincs PE9 1XP

PRINTING
Gomer Press Limited, Llandysul Ceredigion, South Wales.

ADVERTISING
Advertising: Gemma Gray
Email: gemma.gray@keypublishing.com
Tel: 01780 755131 **Fax:** 01780 757261
Advertising Production: Rebecca Duffy
Tel: 01780 755131
Fax: 01780 757261
Email: rebecca.duffy@keypublishing.co.uk

PUBLISHING
Publisher: Adrian Cox
Tel: 01780 755131
Fax: 01780 757261
Email: adrian.cox@keypublishing.com

Executive Chairman: Richard Cox
Managing Director: Adrian Cox
Commercial Director: Ann Saundry
Sales & Marketing Manager: Martin Steele

 Key Publishing Ltd,
Units 1-4, Gwash Way Industrial Estate
Ryhall Road Stamford, Lincs PE9 1XP

Welcome

Four years since we completed Twelve Trees Junction - and following two years in storage - we relaunched our big Southern Region layout at the Great Electric Train Show this year with a new storage yard and extended scenery. Read the full story on pages 72-79.

WELCOME TO THE 2018 *Hornby Magazine Yearbook* which celebrates the highlights of 2017, the expectations for 2018 and *Hornby Magazine's* 10th anniverary year too. And what a year it has been - 60 new model releases, a dramatic rise in interest towards 'O' gauge, 36 stunning feature layouts in our pages, hundreds of hours spent in our workshop creating models for the magazine and shows - and it only seems like yesterday when we were finishing work on Grosvenor Square for Yearbook No. 9.

This hobby is incredibily busy - blink for a moment and something will pass you by, be that a weekend exhibition, new announcement or latest release. The good news is we are watching everything like a hawk keeping check on model production so that we can bring you the latest reviews, layouts and show information as quickly as they happen. And, better still, if you missed anything there is a high chance you are about to read about it in this Yearbook.

This year we have moved the format of the Yearbook on from previous years and a layout project isn't at the centre of what we have put together. Instead we've looked back on the highlights of the year and brought together features which take those new releases, products and anniversaries further with brand new material throughout. This includes features looking at the array of shunting locomotives now available, rejuvenating Hornby's long standing model of the BR ferry van for 'OO', tackling wagon kit construction in three scales and exploring the possibilities of modelling 'Motorail' traffic.

Allied to that our resident historian Evan Green-Hughes has been hard at work to deliver two stand out features on the real railway covering the development of the most glamourous of steam locomotives - the 'Pacifics' - as well as going back to the late 1980s to recall the changing face of Railfreight at sectorisation.

Of course our Yearbook wouldn't be complete without a project layout, but we've done it differently this time. Instead of building something from scratch we've gone down the route of rebuilding our flagship 'OO' Southern Region layout Twelve Trees Junction to make it more usable at exhibitions while also expanding its scenic content. If you were at the Great Electric Train Show we hope you enjoyed seeing what we have done (so far) and I can tell you that there is a lot more to come on this layout in the future. We'll be showcasing the next steps in the pages of future issues of *Hornby Magazine*.

2017 has flown by in an instant, but that is, I think, because it has been such an impressive year for model railway production. It feels like we've seen more variety, a greater desire to embrace new technology and to develop models which are a cut above the rest. Part of that comes from the increased competition from new names in ready-to-run, some of which are pushing the boundaries for what we can expect from future models including the RealTrack Models Class 156.

We hope you enjoy our 10th annual Yearbook as much as we have enjoyed creating the models and writing the features that you find inside. This incredible hobby shows no signs of slowing and with the impressive list of new products still to come, it really can only get better.

Happy modelling!

Mike Wild
Mike Wild
Editor, *Hornby Magazine*

HORNBY magazine TOP 20 OF 2017

Picking a single standout product from the past year is near impossible with so many contenders - and for many different reasons - so we won't. Instead, in our second annual feature, *Hornby Magazine* highlights **20 OF THE BEST** which we have reviewed or worked with during the past 12 months.

1 Hornby Peckett 'W4' 0-4-0ST

■ www.hornby.com ■ **£87.99** ■ **'OO' gauge**

Hornby's tiny Peckett 'W4' 0-4-0ST took the modelling world by storm even before it had arrived. It is amongst the smallest ready-to-run steam locomotives to be produced for the 'OO' scale market – only the Lancashire & Yorkshire Railway 'Pug' 0-4-0ST comes close – and has a charm which won over thousands of would-be purchasers to the point that it was sold out before it arrived in the shops.

Happily, Hornby realised this appeal and it is making a return again in 2017 in black and in 2018 in two new green industrial liveries. Three made up the initial batch which landed in the final weeks of 2016 covering Peckett green as 563 *Dodo*, Manchester Ship Canal No. 11 in dark green and Huntley and Palmer blue as locomotive 'D'.

Its compact size belies the fact that this is a powerful little locomotive with space for conversion to digital control with Hornby's X9659 four-pin decoder. In fact, we went as far as to install digital sound in this tiny locomotive using a Zimo MX648 decoder, neat wiring and a reduced size 8mm x 12mm cube speaker in HM117.

Simply superb.

DCC Concepts alignment dowels

■ www.dccconcepts.com ■ **£16.96** ■ **All scales**

2

Sometimes, it's the simple things which really catch our attention and nowhere is that truer than with these alignment dowels by DCC Concepts. This manufacturer is renowned for its top-quality products and these are no exception. We've used them on four layouts now, and we won't build another portable layout without them – they are that good. Instant alignment of baseboards every time is their ability and you can even buy a kit containing all the drill bits you require as well.

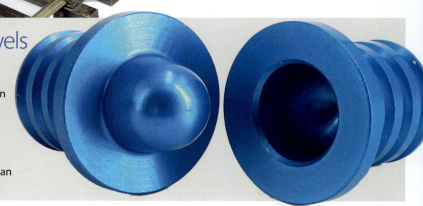

Masterpiece Figures

- 01428 727341
- From £5 (unpainted)
- 'OO' gauge

3 Locomotive footplates are an area we often forget to populate, but a bare cab of a moving steam locomotive really does look quite odd. For several years now we've been using Masterpiece Figures footplate crews and its range of unpainted and painted figures continues to grow. The manufacturer produces different poses for a range of locomotives so even if you have a pair of identical 'Pacifics' the crews can be at work in different positions. Simple to fit, designed specifically for ready-to-run locomotives and neatly painted, these are hard to beat as a simple, quick and effective means of populating your cabs.

4

Little Loco Co BTH Class 15

- www.littleloco.co.uk
- £375
- 'O' gauge

This newcomer to the British 'O' gauge ready-to-run market scored a hit with its first release – the British Thompson Houston Class 15 Bo-Bo diesel. Beautifully finished, smooth running and with impressive detail features, it set a new standard in ready-to-run 'O' gauge diesel locomotives.

Its specification includes factory-fitted speakers in all models, a Plux22 decoder socket, independently controlled headlights on DCC, cab lighting, cab interior detail, a DCC sound option from the factory using a Zimo decoder and impressive engine and braking controls and much more.

Little Loco Co released the model in January 2017 in BR green, BR green with small yellow warning panels and BR green with full yellow ends. Each came with a transfer sheet to allow it to be personalised with the owner's choice of running number too.

In all respects this is a standout product showing new potential and design ethos for 'O' gauge diesel models.

5

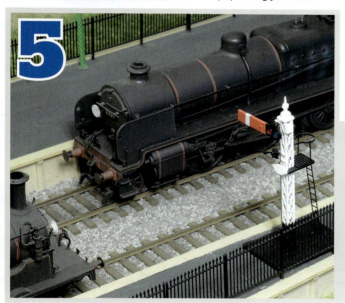

Dapol lattice post signal

- www.dapol.co.uk
- £30.45
- 'OO' gauge

Dapol's range of ready built signals has continued to grow and in last year's Yearbook we highlighted the Southern Railway rail built signals. This year an even more attractive signal has been released in the London & South Western Railway lattice post signal. This impressively intricate signal has a refinement that would be hard to build from a kit and we have been totally impressed by its operation under digital control. Dapol has also updated its installation notes for these signals, particularly in respect of power supplies to maintain their reliable operation. A great signal for the end of the platform.

6

Graham Farish sound fitted 'N' gauge 'Castle'

- www.bachmann.co.uk
- £219.95
- 'N' gauge

Digital sound has become a new focus for Bachmann's 'N' gauge Graham Farish range. Following on from the success of its Class 108 Diesel Multiple Unit with sound (HM Yearbook No. 9) it released the all-new 'Castle' in May 2017 and followed it with a factory sound fitted version. Not only does it look superb, but the sound quality and drivability of the Zimo controlled sound version was outstanding.

The 'Castle' was also the first of the 'N' gauge range to be released with a Next18 decoder socket - the replacement of the earlier and more limited 6-pin plug – and the design is now being rolled out across all new production models with its next release being the Class 40.

The sound fitted 'Castle' is a brilliant little model with tons of Great Western charm.

7 Kernow Bulleid's 1-Co-Co-1 diesel

■ www.kernowmodelrailcentre.com ■ £169.99 ■ 'OO' gauge

This makes our top 20 not just for what it represents, but also because it is Kernow Model Rail Centre's first solo product produced direct with a factory in China and

for the stir it caused when we had a pre-production sample running on Grosvenor Square at the Great Central Railway Model Event in June 2017.

This impressive 16-wheeled 1-Co-Co-1 diesel was the forerunner of the Class 40 and three were built to Bulleid's design by British Railways – two in 1950 and a third

in 1954. Kernow's model caters for differences between the real locomotives and is a stunning must-have model of these sought after prototype diesels.

Dapol's Vossloh Class 68

■ www.dapol.co.uk ■ £145.55 ■ 'OO' gauge

8 Modern diesel locomotives aren't known for the quality of their soundtrack, but the new Vossloh built Class 68s operated by Direct Rail Services, ScotRail and Chilterns Trains have attracted quite a following for their ability to make the 'right' noise.

In April 2017 Dapol released its eagerly awaited model of the

new Class 68 for 'OO' gauge and, while there was a fault with the DRS version which has since been corrected with new bodyshells, it was a stand out model of the year.

Modelling a brand new locomotive is a challenge in itself, especially as Dapol started developing the '68' while the real locomotives were under

construction. Still, the end result was an impressively powerful smooth running locomotive which has an impressive array of lighting functions too.

Hornby's air-smoothed 'Merchant Navy'

■ www.hornby.com ■ £189.99 ■ 'OO' gauge

9 For the Southern Region modellers, one of the biggest missing links was the original condition air-smoothed 'Merchant Navy' 4-6-2, but in Spring 2017 that gap was filled with the arrival of Hornby's brand new model of the class of 30.

With so many variations between the locomotives, producing the 'MN' was something of a challenge, but Hornby's development team rose to the occasion by delivering a model which can be produced with some 180 different combinations of parts to create almost every single one of the fleet at any time in its

air-smoothed career.

Perhaps most stylish is the sell-out model of 21C1 *Channel Packet* in as-built condition, but Hornby was also quick to deliver versions as 21C3 *Royal Mail* in Southern Railway malachite green as well

as BR built examples as 35023 *Holland-Afrika Line* (with Twin Track Sound) and as the erstwhile 35028 *Clan Line*, both finished in British Railway lined green.

The 'Merchant Navy' is a stunning example of modern

model technology and the manufacturer's ability to recreate all the minor and major variations which took place during a class's career. Excellent and soon new versions will be coming through with the 2018 catalogue.

The first production sample touched down in the *Hornby Magazine* office just in time to make it into this Yearbook with the full supply expected during November.

We've since spent a full weekend operating this locomotive at the Great Electric Train Show where the public response was nothing short of amazing.

11
Kernow's 4-TC unit

- www.kernowmodelrailcentre.com
- £289.95
- 'OO' gauge

This had to be in the top 20 – Kernow Model Rail Centre's (KMRC) gorgeous 'OO' gauge model of the BR 4-TC trailer control unit.

Touching down in September 2017 with the Cornish retailer, this unit has caused something of a stir because, even though it is correct, it isn't powered. However, we think KMRC has been quite clever as they have served up a go-anywhere Southern Region multiple unit which was seen both across the ex-London & South Western Railway main line from London to Weymouth as well as on duties taking the fleet to places as far from the Southern as Birmingham and Cardiff. Plus you can run it with Class 33s, 71s and 73s for good measure.

All in all, this is a well thought out product which adds to the range of Southern third-rail units. If you own a Class 33/1 or 73 you need at least one of these!

10
Bachmann Webb 'Coal Tank'

- www.bachmann.co.uk
- £119.95
- 'OO' gauge

With the mainstream seemingly very well catered for, manufacturers are increasingly looking towards pre-grouping steam locomotive designs to fulfil the demands of new ready-to-run products and especially in 'OO' gauge.

Victorian era locomotives have an appeal all of their own and some hold a special place in railway history for their longevity including the Webb 'Coal Tank' which was released by Bachmann after a long gestation in May 2017. Interestingly, even though the class only ever carried black as the livery base colour from London North Western Railway to British Railways days, this venerable 0-6-2T design caught everyone's attention.

Bachmann's 'Birdcage' stock

12
- www.bachmann.co.uk
- £59.95 per coach
- 'OO' gauge

Bachmann's 'OO' gauge South Eastern and Chatham Railway (SECR) 'Birdcage' stock has been a long time coming, but the result is well worth the wait. These attractive carriages which date back to the 1910s touched down in British Railways crimson livery, but are due for release in SECR and Southern Railway schemes too.

Superbly finished and well appointed in all respects.

DCC Concepts Cobalt IP point motor

- www.dccconcepts.com
- £19.95 each
- All scales

13
If there is one product we recommend more than any other then it has to be the DCC Concepts Cobalt IP point motor. These latest generation point motors from DCC Concepts are at the top of the game. They may not be the cheapest, but often you get what you pay for and that is certainly true here.

As well as offering a rapid installation time – under five minutes per motor in our experience, including wiring connections – these robustly built DCC fitted versions of the Cobalt motor are incredibly simple to install, come with a built in decoder with quick programming and setup options and have frog switching, feedback and switch operation connection for points too.

We've installed more than 100 of these motors and they have proved reliable on our exhibition layouts time after time. Highly recommended.

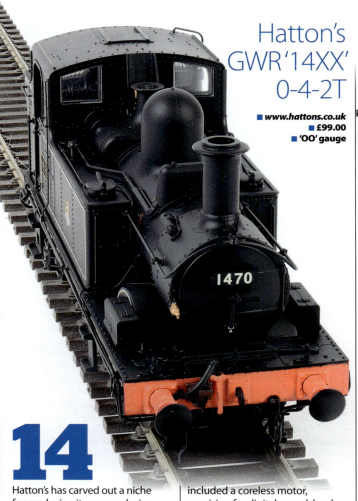

Hatton's GWR '14XX' 0-4-2T

- www.hattons.co.uk
- £99.00
- 'OO' gauge

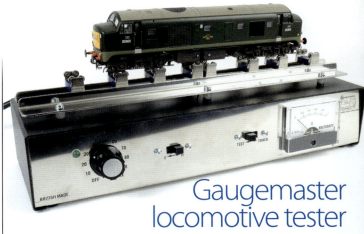

Gaugemaster locomotive tester

- www.gaugemaster.com ∎ £299.95 ∎ 'N'-'P4'

15 It's all too easy to be swayed by the latest new locomotive, carriage or wagon, but during 2017 Gaugemaster released this useful locomotive tester and controller. It is supplied with a set of DCC Concepts rolling road rollers which means that by adjusting the rail positions it can

be used to test 'N', 'OO9', 'TT', 'HO', 'OO', 'EM' and 'P4' locomotives to name just a few. Plus it can be switched to drive trains on a layout too. We have found this to be an invaluable product in the *Hornby Magazine* office for running in new locomotive models before they are set to work on our test track. Highly recommend to both analogue and digital layout owners.

14 Hatton's has carved out a niche for producing its own exclusive products and during 2017 has even moved to work directly with factories in China to deliver its 'Warwell' bogie wagons as well as its recently announced SECR 'P' 0-6-0T and Andrew Barclay 0-4-0ST.

However, its best product for 2017 was definitely the DJ Models produced exclusive model of the GWR '14XX' 0-4-2T family which included versions of the '48XX' and '58XX' derivatives too. Highlights

included a coreless motor, provision for digital sound, hook for the dummy front coupling, a removable smokebox door for access to the decoder socket and a correctly modelled BR smokebox numberplate with supports on the smokebox door.

Operating as well as it looked, this all-new version of the Collett 0-4-2T is a fitting addition to any Great Western or Western Region layout both main line and branch line.

Zimo 3D printed speakers

- www.zimo.at
- From £11.00
- 'OO' and upwards

16 The unseen can often have a massive impact, and that is certainly true of Zimo's new line of baffled speakers with 3D printed enclosures. These have taken its range of cube

speakers into a new league by offering twin driver units ready built for installation as well as larger single units with baffles to increase their performance. Once inside a locomotive, you will never see them, but they make a tremendous difference to the sound output of decoders.

'N' gauge Hawksworth Autocoach

- www.bachmann.co.uk ∎ £34.95 ∎ 'N' gauge

The Great Western Railway's auto trains were a brilliant feature of its branch line operations which are perfectly suited to compact model railways. In April 2017 Graham Farish

released its all new Hawksworth autocoach which acts as the perfect partner to its 2016 model of the GWR '64XX' 0-6-0PT which made it into our top 20 of 2016.

First released in BR carmine and cream and BR lined maroon liveries, this new autocoach came with a superbly modelled body, interior detail, separate parts to

detail the bufferbeam and even a lamp to add to the carriage front too. An excellent addition to the Graham Farish steam era carriage portfolio.

17

18

Dapol 'O' gauge BR 12ton box vans

■ www.dapol.co.uk ■ £49.95 ■ 'O' gauge

The BR 12ton box van is the type of vehicle that any layout set between 1950 and the mid-1970s can't be without. They were universal in goods trains throughout the country and could be seen from the far north of Scotland to the deepest recesses of the Cornish branch network.

In 2017 Dapol released its new model of the BR 12ton box van for 'O' gauge, satisfying a market which can't get enough of them. The first

batch sold out from Dapol before it arrived in the UK and a second run was quickly issued and this arrived in the late summer. Four versions have now been released covering planked and plywood sided standard 12ton vans, an insulated 10ton van and, most recently, the 12ton meat van. In addition, you can choose from a selection of five-plank open wagons while there will soon be a 'Vanwide' to add to freight trains in 'O' gauge.

19

Heljan Class B tanker

■ www.heljan.dk ■ £24.95 ■ 'OO' gauge

In April 2017 Heljan delivered what can easily be described as its best ready-to-run 'OO' gauge wagon so far in the Class B four-wheel 35ton tanker. Famed for their use in block oil trains from Fawley near Southampton, these popular vehicles were introduced in 1957 to provide a higher capacity means of moving oil around the railway network.

Heljan's model has been released in the always popular Esso black livery as well as United Molasses, Regent and Mobil schemes and was quickly followed by the Class A (petroleum tanker) of a similar vintage and style. If you missed out, further batches are planned for release to make up realistic 1960s era block oil workings.

Realtrack's Class 156

■ www.realtrackmodels.co.uk
■ £210.00
■ 'OO' gauge

20

Realtrack Models might not be the most familiar name in 'OO' gauge ready-to-run, but with its current performance for delivering high value products like the new Class 156, it soon will be.

Realtrack first appeared with its FLA container flat twin sets and then took the multiple unit world by storm with its Class 143/144 'Pacer' DMUs. However, the new '156' is

better yet with a low profile drive mechanism which is totally invisible from the outside, full depth interior mouldings, cleverly hidden decoder socket positions, impressive lighting function options on digital control and a standard of detailing second to none.

The underframes alone are reported to have more separate parts in than the entire original Lima version of the Class 156 – although we haven't counted. It is clear to see that much time, knowledge and skill have been invested in creating what can only be seen as the best Diesel Multiple Unit to be made to date for 'OO'.

Read our full round up of 2016-2017 new product releases on pages 96-103.

'PACIFIC' *Power vs*

2017 has seen the arrival of two significant models from Hornby in the air-smoothed 'Merchant Navy' and a brand-new model of the Stanier 'Duchess' for 'OO'. *Hornby Magazine* puts these two giants of steam head to head.

WITH THEIR IMPOSING power, grand names and dedication to the fastest express trains, 'Pacifics' have always been the most sought-after locomotives in model form. In these days of exotic and historic steam locomotive models for the ready-to-run market it is becoming increasingly rare that we see two of the most glamorous locomotives turned out in one year. 2017 though has seen the arrival of the missing link for the 'Pacific' story in Hornby's air-smoothed 'Merchant Navy' 4-6-2 for the Southern Region in 'OO' and most recently its all new model of the Stanier 'Duchess' 4-6-2 for the Midland Region.

The 'Duchess' has been a long-standing part of the Hornby catalogue, the first being produced by Hornby Dublo in 1948, and most recently we have become accustomed to the 2001 released

model. However, it must be said that we weren't quite prepared for just how good this all-new model looks in the flesh. We'd seen the pictures but, quite frankly, they just hadn't done it justice.

On the other hand, we have the 'Merchant Navy' in its original air-smoothed form – a locomotive which modellers have been crying out for in 'OO' gauge and one which fills a big gap in the market. Moreover, Hornby really has gone to town on this complicated fleet of 30 locomotives by developing a tooling suite which, in combination with liveries, means it has 180 options available to release on this 4-6-2 in the future.

Power vs efficiency

These two locomotive classes had very different places in railway history. Stanier's 'Duchess' was pure power. Its four-cylinder layout, large and free steaming boiler and wide firebox gave it everything it needed to be a force to be reckoned

PARADE
efficiency

with on even the heaviest West Coast Main Line expresses. To put it into context, double heading was required with early diesels to match the power of a 'Duchess'. Only the advent of electrification allowed a single locomotive to replace them.

The class of 38 locomotives was introduced in 1937 at a time when speed, journey times and publicity were of the utmost importance

and Stanier's employer, the London Midland & Scottish Railway (LMS), was head to head with the London and North Eastern Railway (LNER) to get from London to Scotland the quickest. The 'Duchess' was rivalled by Gresley's mighty streamlined 'A4' 4-6-2 and, in a bid for publicity, the first of Stanier's 'Duchess' class, or 'Princess Coronations', were delivered with streamlining too. It was all about the glamour, the publicity »

Single and double chimney options

Die-cast metal chassis for adhesion

Powerful five-pole motor

and making a name for the railway.

The Second World War and safety put paid to any more exploits with speed, particularly after a near miss at Crewe where on a publicity run 6220 *Coronation* approached the pointwork too fast and nearly caused a disaster. It was reported as achieving 114mph that day and there was no questioning the power of these stunning locomotives which have been reported as making over 3,000hp at the cylinders – more than any diesels of their time other than the 3,300hp 'Deltics'.

Fortunately, three have been saved for preservation with 46235 *City of Birmingham* housed at the Thinktank, Birmingham Science Museum in its

namesake city, 46233 *Duchess of Sutherland* in service with the Princess Royal Class Locomotive Trust and operating on the national network and, of course, 6229 *Duchess of Hamilton* which has been restreamlined as part of its ongoing position of importance in the National Railway Museum in York alongside speed record holding Gresley 'A4' 4-6-2 4468 *Mallard*.

Fast forward three years to 1941 and, miraculously, the Southern Railway's flamboyant Chief Mechanical Engineer Oliver Bulleid managed to achieve the impossible by having production of his radical new 'Merchant Navy' class 'Pacifics' signed off at the height of the Second World War. While construction of express

locomotives was banned, Bulleid convinced the authorities that these were to be mixed-traffic locomotives, and got permission to build them. The truth when it came to their typical duties was rather different.

These locomotives were to efficiency and steam age technology what the 'Duchess' was to power. They were a departure from convention in almost every way with their 'air-smoothed' casing bringing about an image which stood out from the crowd. Beneath the skin they were just as radical with a cab designed for efficiency from the crew perspective – steam operated firebox doors and electric lighting inside and out - Bulleid Firth-Brown pattern wheels for weight saving, chain-driven valve gear, and a boiler and firebox using all welded construction and a claimed thermal efficiency over conventional design. They had a three-cylinder layout with the motion chain driven and encased in an oil bath. They were a radical leap forward.

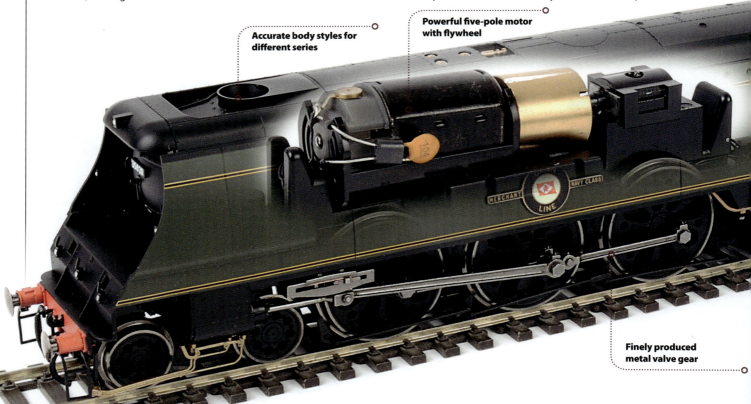

Accurate body styles for different series

Powerful five-pole motor with flywheel

Finely produced metal valve gear

Space for a 28mm round speaker and 8-pin decoder

A fleet of 30 was eventually built with 21C1 *Channel Packet* entering traffic in 1941. There were many revisions to the design as Bulleid revised and adjusted his outstanding creation, but the last weren't constructed until after nationalisation. However, they were masters of their trade and once on the move – Bulleid's 'Pacifics' being renowned for slipping on starting – they could match the acceleration of Electric Multiple Units (EMUs) on stopping trains, even at the head of heavy West of England expresses.

Such innovations came at a cost, as the fleet was found to be rather unreliable, which ultimately led British Railways to rebuild the entire class in more conventional form, removing the air-smoothed casing and complex chain driven valve gear, but retaining the efficient and powerful boiler. In this form the 'Merchant Navies' reached their potential. The last wasn't withdrawn until the very last day of steam operation on the Southern Region on July 9 1967.

Incredibly, 11 of the 30 have been preserved and six of those have steamed in preservation, although currently 35006 *Peninsular and Oriental Line*, 35018 *British India Line* and 35028 *Clan Line* are active, with the latter two registered for main line operation.

The models

Hornby's models of these two giants of the steam era are stunning replicas. Both perform to an exemplary level with high powered five-pole motors delivering ample haulage capacity. The detailing invested in each is phenomenal and it is clear that the 'Duchess' is going be regarded as the best of its type in mass-production - it will even cater for the final two Ivatt 'Duchesses' which had modifications beneath the cab and to the trailing bogie.

As locomotives go, they don't get much more iconic or appealing as these two stunning machines and with their compatibility with Digital Command Control and provision for speaker installation they are simple to take to the next level should you wish to do so.

The 'Merchant Navy' made its debut in March 2017 as 21C1 *Channel Packet* (Cat No. R3434) and 21C3 *Royal Mail* (R3435) in Southern Railway malachite green as well as in British Railways lined green with early crests as 35023 *Holland-Afrika Line* (R3382XTTS) and 35028 *Clan Line* (R3436). All of those were sell-out successes for Hornby, but happily there are more versions coming in 2018.

The 'Duchess' was literally just around the corner in early October as this Yearbook closed for press and the first were due to be in the shops during that month. On release it will be available as 6231 *Duchess of Atholl* in LMS lined crimson without smoke deflectors (R3553), 46235 *City of Birmingham* in BR lined green with late crests and Twin Track Sound (R3509TTS) and as 46256 *Sir William A Stanier FRS* in BR lined maroon with late crests (R3555).

If you have been looking for a 'Pacific', which do you choose? Really it is down to personal preference and your modelling area. Based on their outstanding quality, though, many modellers will want both (as I do!). That, surely, is testament to the quality of design and production which has been invested in the two locomotives you see here. ■

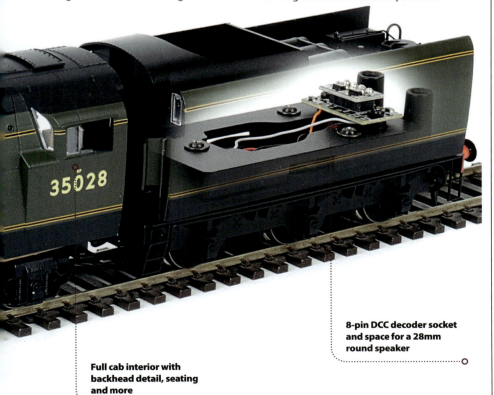

8-pin DCC decoder socket and space for a 28mm round speaker

Full cab interior with backhead detail, seating and more

35 WAYS TO BUILD A...
BETTER MODEL RAILWAY

Building a model railway is a rewarding experience, but where do you start and what do you need to know? **MIKE WILD** offers a collection of 35 tips, techniques and products to make your project even better.

Building a model railway is a great experience. This is *Hornby Magazine's* **Barrenthorpe, modelled in 'N' gauge, shortly after completion of its rebuild for the Great Electric Train Show in 2016. A Stanier 'Duchess' 4-6-2 dominates the scene as it overtakes a BR '9F' 2-10-0 on a cement working. On the left a Class 121 is held at the signal while the depot is busy in the background.**
Mike Wild/*Hornby Magazine*.

DESIGN AND CONSTRUCTION

1 Plan it!

Planning is a fun part of creating a model railway. It's a time to indulge and consider your options. We've spent hundreds of hours designing model railways which will never be built, but usually they include a feature that we can or will build into a project at some stage in the future. Having a clear plan of what you will build helps to keep a layout under control too. You can decide on baseboard sizes and shapes at an early stage with planning and this really helps.

2 Research

Visit model and book shops, look around when you travel by train and take in your surroundings. If you are aiming to model a real location, visit it with your camera and take photographs. Remember that to build a model railway we can't just focus on the railway – we need to look at the area it is in too.

3 Choose a region

It is your railway and you can run it how you wish, but making a choice of region will save your bank balance from being overstretched with every new release. This goes hand in hand with researching a layout. Still, if you can't decide there are plenty of places where two regions operate so you can indulge in more than one.

4 Choose your scale

There are three primary scales, all with subsidiaries, from which to choose: 'OO', 'N' and 'O' gauge. Which one suits you comes down to the space you have and how much you want to invest as much as the availability of rolling stock. All three of the main scales are now well supplied with quality ready-to-run products as well as a vast support network of specialist suppliers. There are finescale equivalents of each of these, but these take much more time, patience and skill than the standard scales. Also worth a look is 'OO9' narrow gauge – 4mm scale trains running on 9mm gauge track – with the promise of new ready-to-run products from Bachmann and Heljan before the end of 2017.

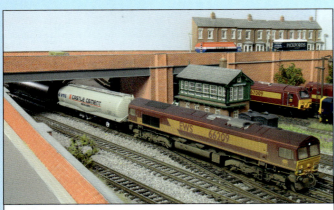

5 Choose an era

Selecting an era isn't just for rolling stock – it links to the whole feel of a model railway. A brand new 2017 Scania articulated lorry will look very out of place next to a 1957 period British Railways station and choosing an era and sticking to it will keep a layout looking realistic.

6 Choose a location

Decide where you are going to build your layout. Do you have a spare room ready to use? Can it go in the garage? What about building a dedicated shed in the garden or converting the loft? Could you build a garden railway? If none of these work for you then why not think about joining a model railway club where you can be part of much bigger projects?

7 Think laterally

You don't have to be constrained by walls. Building a big exhibition layout can be great fun, although challenging, and while you might only be able to run it at shows there is nothing better than taking your pride and joy out to show an eager public. For example, our current project Twelve Trees Junction is 24ft x 10ft and we can't assemble the full layout indoors at the workshop – that hasn't stopped us though as you can see.

8 Plan your train lengths

Knowing what length trains you want versus what train lengths will fit on your layout are two important factors. If you decide you want eight coach trains you need to build a big layout to fit them on – and include suitable loops at stations to support them. Equally, if branch line trains are your interest you can save a lot of space. These choices will affect your trackplan greatly.

9 Use the right materials

We have three recommendations when it comes to baseboard materials: 9mm plywood for the tops and 70mm x 18mm planed timber for the framework. Using these has created solid and reliable baseboards for *Hornby Magazine's* layouts time and time again. Our third material of choice is 6mm Medium Density Fibreboard (MDF) for backscenes – its smooth finish makes it perfect for creating neat backdrops. Don't be tempted to use it for baseboard tops though – MDF spells problems if you do that.

10 Use the right tools

As simple as it sounds, using the wrong tool or, just as bad, a blunt tool can make the process of construction arduous. If your saw is worn, replace it with a new one and if your craft knife blade is blunt, replace it. Small things like this make a huge difference to the pleasure of layout construction.

11 Alignment dowels work

If your layout needs to be dismantled for storage or transport then we highly recommend the use of alignment dowels. Fitting these means that each time a layout is assembled the tracks line up as they should every time. We have standardised on DCC Concepts dowels – they are simple to fit and the results are phenomenal, saving a great deal of time and energy in aligning baseboards.

12 If you can't do it find someone who can

Model railway construction is a multi-skilled project – you need to have basic knowledge of woodwork, track laying, electrics, painting, art and more. But you don't have to be able to do everything yourself. If you can't build baseboards, try looking into baseboard kits such as those by Tim Horn – *www.timhorn. co.uk* - or if you want baseboards built to order you can try White Rose Model Works – *www. whiterosemodelworks.co.uk* - or one of the many other board builders.

This extends further: if you are going to build your own boards, get the timber supplier to cut the sheet material to size, it will save a lot of time and effort and make transporting the sheet materials home much easier.

TRACK AND OPERATION

13 Go digital!

If you are starting a brand new layout, digital is the way to go. It offers a stunning level of control of locomotives, rolling stock and accessories and opens up the potential for a totally engrossing experience including sound. It will take research to decide on a system, but once you go digital you won't go back.

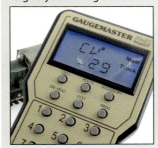

14 Join track neatly

Making a neat join between lengths of track is essential for a reliable model railway. Joining set track pieces is straightforward, but always ensure that both rail joiners are pushed fully onto the adjoining piece. If you are using flexible track, trimming the rail chairs off the leading sleeper will allow rail joiners to sit between it and the rail comfortably. Repeat the process on the adjacent piece for a join which is virtually invisible.

15 Test it!

This is the fun part – every time you add a new feature, loop or section of track, test it. It's the most rewarding part of model railway construction seeing a train run. It's also wise to run a variety of trains through newly laid track to ensure everything behaves as it should.

16 Make it live

If you are going to go digital, then you should make your layout live. This means that all of the track is fed power from the controller at all times, even sidings and loops. Locomotive lights will stay on even when the points are set against them while sounds can be kept on too. It takes a little planning and a few extra wiring connections, but it is worthwhile.

17 Use underlay

This has multiple purposes. It provides a modicum of sound deadening, but in pursuit of building a realistic railway it will also help to create a realistic ballast shoulder around the running lines. We use 1/16in thick cork bought in rolls for 'OO' gauge layouts, but there are other good choices out there including Woodland Scenics Trackbed which can be bought in strips and sheets.

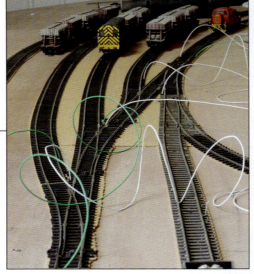

18 Wiring code

When wiring a model railway, develop a code for your wiring. Using one colour for everything is bound to result in disaster just as much as using random odds and ends to finish the job. We standardise on red for left rail, black for right rail, green and orange for point motors with white for the common return on solenoids.

19 Learn to solder

Soldering is an essential skill for model railway construction, much of which comes from using the right tools and materials. We use an Antex 25watt soldering iron with a 2mm bit and standard 1mm diameter electrical solder for track connections. Always ensure the iron is hot before using it and avoid extended contact between the nib and rail sides/wires in all circumstances.

20 Prepare for point motors - now

If there is even a remote chance that you will add point motors in the future, drill the holes for them at the track laying stage – it will be a lot harder once all the track is down and more so if you have started scenery. A 9mm drill bit will create a hole large enough for virtually any commercially available point motor and provide enough space for the arm to move with 'OO', 'N' and 'O' gauge points – just mark the centre with a 1mm drill through the tie bar of the point before using the larger drill.

21 Use the right wire

Using the right type of wire is just as important as setting a colour code. We use 7/0.2 (seven strands of 0.2 diameter wire) multi-core wire for track connections and 42/0.2 wire for power bus wiring on digital layouts. This combination has given reliable service on our layouts repeatedly.

22 Plan for accessories

Most layouts develop in stages and it's unlikely that you will want to go through all the process at once. Having a plan for the future will mean you can go back and add extra features such as lighting, signalling and more without having to undo existing modelling. This can be as simple as ensuring there is space under the board for wiring or space alongside the track for that extra feature you want to add one day.

23 Consider your curves

Most ready-to-run locomotives and rolling stock are designed for a minimum of second radius curves – that's 438mm or 17 ¼in radius. However, with some steam locomotives, once you fit items such as steps and bufferbeam details this can restrict their ability on sharp curves. Aim for the widest possible curves, but keep them down to a minimum of second radius.

24 Leave space around the railway

Don't be tempted to fill every corner and void on the baseboards with track. It might be fun at first, but your layout will soon look unrealistic and over-populated. Leaving space around the railway will allow you to indulge in scenic modelling too.

DETAILING AND SCENERY

25 Tone it down

Toning down your freshly laid track with a coat of weathering will instantly transform the bright fresh metal into a more realistic railway. We use Humbrol No. 29 from an aerosol for a quick base coat being careful to mask point blades before spraying. This acts to coat the rail sides as well as the sleepers and gives a muted tone. Using bright rust orange colours doesn't look right on well used rails.

26 Blend your ballast

Ballast in the real world isn't one consistent colour or size – it has variations. We use Woodland Scenics medium and fine grade blended grey ballasts (Cat Nos. B1393 and B1394) to ballast *Hornby Magazine's* layouts. The two are mixed in a pot before applying to the layout for a varied finish to the track ballasting.

27 Learn to airbrush

An airbrush is an essential tool in scenic modelling just as much as it is in painting and weathering rolling stock. And in fact, scenic modelling is the perfect place to start as the basic skills of operating an airbrush can be learnt while applying colour to track. Once you have learnt how to use an airbrush you will find it to be an invaluable tool in all areas of railway modelling from painting rolling stock to adding the finishing touches to a building or structure.

28 Static grass

There is no better way of adding relief to grassed areas than static grass. This clever material stands on end when a static charge is applied to it and is available in a bewildering array of colours, shades and lengths. We've used the MiniNatur and Green Scene static grass ranges with great success on *Hornby Magazine's* layouts – all applied with a Noch Grasmaster device. The most expensive part is the Grasmaster, but, at the price of a ready-to-run tank engine, it produces grass effects which will stand proud alongside today's impressive rolling stock.

29 Fine leaf foliage

It might not be cheap, but Woodland Scenics Fine Leaf Foliage is an absolute must in our scenery armoury. This ready coloured, ready to plant material is a perfect means of adding small bushes, bedding buildings and structures into the ground and creating small trees. It can be broken down into small pieces or used as large chunks and comes in several shades for variety too.

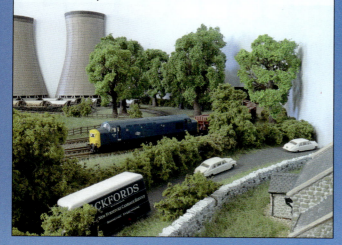

30 Glue buildings down first

Before you start on scenery, decide on where your buildings will go in each area to be developed, complete any detailing you might want to do and then glue them direct to the baseboard or landscape. This will help to bed them into the scene while gluing them on top of ground cover materials will leave an uneven join between the building and the ground.

31 Be consistent

Learn which manufacturers' scenic products you like working with and use them across the layout – the consistency will give the layout a 'joined up' appearance and you can always be sure that the colours will match when you go back to buy more.

32 Add depth and colour

Ground cover, especially grassed areas, gets better with depth and the introduction of colour. Once we've applied static grasses, we go back and work fine and coarse turfs into the basic grass using matt varnish or extra hold hairspray to fix them in place. You can also add a touch of colour with coloured fine turfs to represent flowers growing on bushes and between the grass. Don't overdo it though.

33 Look to Europe and beyond

It's easy to think that European scenic products aren't suitable for British outline layouts, but actually the opposite is true. Noch produces an amazing range of scenic products ranging from ground cover to laser cut detailing items while you would be amazed at how British you can make some of the Walther's American outline kits look. Plus, being American, they make big buildings, something we often lack on model railways.

34 Buy PVA in bulk

PVA - or wood glue - is one of the most versatile glues a modeller can use and you will get through a lot of it in the course of building a model railway. Surprisingly, it is often cheaper, overall, to buy it in a 5 litre tub than a small 1 litre bottle. Its uses stretch from baseboard construction to ballasting, scenery production, adding coal to tenders and more. You will always find another item which can be fixed down with this medium so its well worth keeping on hand.

35 Enjoy it!

The most important tip of all is to enjoy your layout. Keep having running sessions while you build as it will keep the project alive and your interest high.

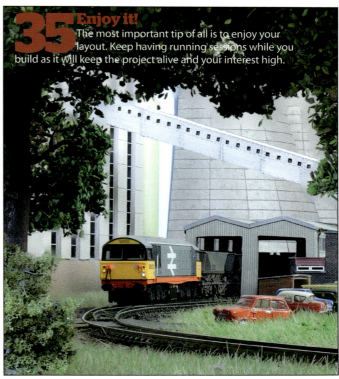

"Through to the British Railways"

For wagon buff **TIM SHACKLETON,** Hornby's relaunch of its 20ton ferry van is a blast from the past. Here he shows you how you can upgrade this landmark model with simple detailing and repainting.

MANUFACTURERS' catalogues of 40-50 years ago were very different to the ones we lust over today. They were much slimmer, for a start, and more like illustrated price lists. But you felt exactly the same excitement when the new issue hit your local model shop, even though there was nothing like the variety of new products we've been used to over the last decade. Once you'd got past the glorious fantasy scene on the cover, it was mostly the same stuff you'd seen in last year's catalogue. It was highly likely the identical products would be there the following year and the year after. That's definitely something that's changed in the interim!

Much of what was on offer in the rolling stock section came under the 'toy' category – there wasn't much that qualified as a 'scale model' as we understand the term nowadays. There was the odd exception, a select number of items that avoided the usual compromises, looked the part

and, in skilled hands, could be turned into a very good model indeed.

As a case in point I've seen some excellent near-scale reworkings of the ancient Tri-ang-Hornby 'Cemflo' (the ones involved in the Thirsk collision of 1967) as well as some convincing revamps of the mighty six-axle 'Trestrol', the Cowans Sheldon hand crane and even Freightliner flats expertly upgraded to create prototypical four-and five-car rakes.

The most promising model of all, I've always felt, was the long-wheelbase ferry van of 1970 vintage – the body was substantially accurate, the details well executed and to my eye this handsome

and imposing model was only let down by its underpinnings, driven by the need to get a 45ft-long van round excruciatingly tight curves.

Now that Hornby has launched an updated, upgraded model incorporating all the benefits of modern Chinese production technology, I thought it might be a plan to pull out some of the older models and see if I could work round their shortcomings to bring them into line with present-day expectations.

As ever, you don't need to follow this process to the letter – you can go a lot further if you like, or you can simply adapt those of my suggestions that meet your own needs. ∎

USEFUL LINKS	
Alan Gibson Workshop	www.alangibsonworkshop.com
Hornby	www.hornby.com
Lifecolor	www.airbrushes.com
Masokits	www.traders.scalefour.org/masokits/
Wizard Models	www.wizardmodels.co.uk
Railtec Transfers	www.railtec-models.com

Continent by

Right: With each upgrade project based around a ready-to-run model or kit, I do an initial audit of what I have and what I hope to achieve. In particular, I ask myself how far I want to go – sometimes the decision is to go for broke, at other times my goal is 'good enough'. The governing factor is usually how much time I want to spend on the model. Cost is a secondary consideration.

Below: With their continental appearance the BR 45ft ferry vans were quite different to other rolling stock and made the journey across the channel by boat. The hooks on the solebar were used to ratchet the vehicles in place on the ferry for the crossing.

Below: The rake of Ferry Vans created here are destined for service on Hornby Magazine's Twelve Trees Junction which will include running behind Hornby's 2016 released Class 71 Bo-Bo electric. Here E5022 heads north from Dover at Twelve Trees with a rake of ten vans.

PART 1
THE CHASSIS

STEP BY STEP **DETAILING AND REPAINTING HORNBY FERRY VANS IN 'OO'**

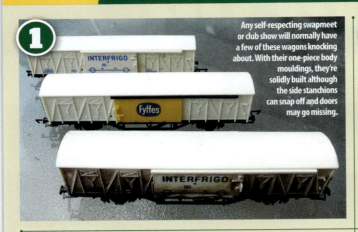

Any self-respecting swapmeet or club show will normally have a few of these wagons knocking about. With their one-piece body mouldings, they're solidly built although the side stanchions can snap off and doors may go missing.

My bargain-basement wagons were quickly broken down into their constituent parts, ready to be rebuilt as BR Continental ferry vans of the 1960s.

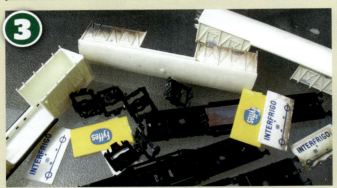

A few minutes later and I've got rid of everything I didn't need, using a circular saw in a mini-drill. I'd shaved off the moulded door detail before realising I could simply remount them with the lettering on the inside.

Compared to this Hornby LNER-pattern CCT, the ferry van rides a scale 6in too high – as did those on many models of the same era. To follow prototype practice, the buffers should align almost exactly, their centres 14mm above the rail.

This is what's causing the height issue – an additional spacer moulded into the underframe. It's easily removed...

...using a cutting burr in my Dremel power tool. Then I'll finish off using this cylindrical grinding attachment to create a perfectly smooth and level finish.

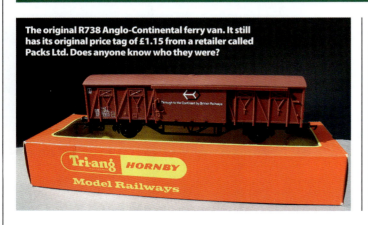

Switching to a circular saw attachment, I've chopped off the door runners and everything else on the chassis relating to the sliding doors. I strongly recommend you wear a respirator mask and eye protection as those tiny fragments of plastic can and do get everywhere – including your eyes and lungs.

FERRY VAN HISTORY

The original R738 Anglo-Continental ferry van. It still has its original price tag of £1.15 from a retailer called Packs Ltd. Does anyone know who they were?

Introduced in 1962, the diagram 1/227 ferry vans were something wholly new on British Railways – long-wheelbase, high-capacity vehicles with both vacuum and air brakes and many features in line with current European practice, such as drop-down ventilators and 15ft wide doors. Delivered in the middle of an economic drive to 'export or die', they were intended for general rail freight traffic on cross-Channel train ferries operating on the Dover-Dunkerque and Harwich-Zeebrugge routes.

In all, some 400 of these 25-tonne vans were built between 1962 and 1964, the first 150 by Pressed Steel in Scotland (B786873–787022) and the remainder by BR at Ashford Works (B787098–787347). All carried 12-digit UIC numbers. Although bauxite livery was universal, there was an intriguing range of lettering styles – early wagons bore 'Through to the Continent by British Railways' graphics with the short-lived 'flying crate' symbol but when the new corporate identity arrived in 1965

Intermediate
Beginner SKILL LEVEL Advanced

8 An excellent guide to details can be found at www.flickr.com/photos/brianews/sets/72157647819117132/ I thinned down some of the more obviously overscale items such as the handbrake levers and cut off the underscale tie-down loops, ready for replacement with etched components. Other features I left well alone because I didn't want to compromise the structural integrity of this critical area. To avoid knife slips and inadvertent damage to the model – and yourself – use a blade that's just past its best.

9 I kept (and even added to) the square trussing instead of ripping it out and replacing it with brass angle. I replaced the chunky brake lever guards, however, with brass strip. Other modifications were limited to what would be visible, in shadow, from a foot or so away. The vacuum cylinders were leftovers from Airfix kits, brake actuators were 'HO' scale mouldings and I made the air tanks from brass tube.

10 Alan Gibson finescale wheels slip comfortably into the Hornby axle units. The brake hangers are white metal castings from the Wizard Models/51L range, glued into slots cut into the plastic mouldings. Remember to remove the moulded-on brake shoes first!

11 On long-wheelbase vehicles such as the ferry van, compensation helps them negotiate tight curves and potentially tricky pointwork. At one end of the chassis the axle units are pinned solidly in place but at the other the wheels maybe need a little latitude. The simplest method is to use one of MJT's cradles, which allow a little up-and-down movement.

12 You can see here how the axle rocks from side to side – it only needs a millimetre or two of movement. The brake shoes are in place and I've checked there's sufficient clearance for the wheels. At the compensated end, I've cut the spring/axlebox assemblies from the plastic axle units and glued them to stubs of styrene hidden behind the solebars.

13 These replacement brass tie-down loops came from Wizard Models/51L. They're inexpensive but make a surprising difference to the refinement of the finished model.

14 The detailed, upgraded underframe looks much more substantial than the original. I've left the clasp brakes unpainted for now so you can see how they add to the solidity of the assembly.

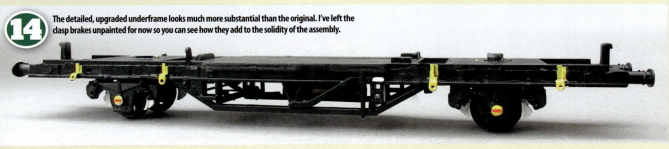

'A new British Railways ferry van showing the wide sliding door which will ease loading and unloading operations' ran the caption to this 1962 press release photograph. B786873 was the first of the Pressed Steel vans to be delivered, and is in the early plain livery carried by initial batches.

this was changed to 'Through to the Continent by British Rail' with a large double-arrow logo. Some were later painted top to toe in bauxite, including underframes, as was the fashion with European-operated ferry vans.

From 1979 onwards many vans received red and grey Railfreight livery with 'Railfreight International' brandings but BR was increasingly reluctant to maintain a large ferry fleet specifically for general traffic to the continent and by 1982 the business of providing stock had largely been handed over to leasing companies. The surviving dual-braked vans, by then coded VIX under TOPS and now minus their UIC numbers, passed to the engineers or found use as barrier wagons, with or without bodywork and in a staggering variety of liveries.

Triang Hornby (as the company then was) had its 'OO' gauge 'Anglo-Continental Ferry Van' out by 1970 and it remained in production for the next decade. Some, as per the prototype, were lettered »

WORKBENCH

STEP BY STEP **DETAILING AND REPAINTING HORNBY FERRY VANS IN 'OO'**

15 Now for the bodywork. The 'ventilator' on the roof is probably something to do with the moulding process. I shaved it off with a scalpel and then rubbed down to a smooth finish.

16 Ditto the handrails and other door furniture. Disposable emery boards are great for this kind of work but don't allow them to become too worn – rather than smoothing down the surface, they're actually roughing it up.

17 I prefer to use a pin vice for precision work such as drilling holes to take the replacement handrails. It gives much greater control than a mini-drill and you won't melt the plastic.

18 To save having to eradicate lettering I didn't want, I turned the doors round and made new grab handles out of 0.45mm hard brass wire, bent to shape with pliers. For strict accuracy, they should be a slightly different shape but I was having one of my lazy days.

19 The rectangular panel on the ends where the body retaining clips sit shouldn't really be there. I carved off the raised rivet detail using a fluted spindle gouge from a set of small woodworking tools. Once the surface had been cleaned up I filled the hole with Evergreen styrene strip and a touch of Squadron green putty. The end framing visible here was modified during the Railfreight era.

20 There's not much else needs doing to the bodyshells. I had thought of breathing a bit of life into the vans by modelling the odd ventilator in the open position – it would have been a challenge but I could only find one photograph showing this, so I didn't in the end. The blue-painted Transfesa vans that brought onions, oranges and other perishables from Spain to Britain often ran with their vents down but I don't think the BR ferry vans were used much for this kind of traffic.

21 Once reassembled, the bodyshells can be airbrush painted as necessary. I used an initial coat of LifeColor Fitted Freight Bauxite (UA817) with Dirty Black (UA731) for the roofs. When dry I sprayed a coat of satin varnish that helps with transfer application. Subsequent weathering will vary the basic colours appreciably.

22 To letter my set of five vans, I used Railtec waterslide transfers throughout – Steve Bell produces them in 2mm, 4mm and 7mm scales. They give you all the intricate little touches that are unique to RIV-registered ferry vehicles.

23 Thanks to Steve's eye for detail, the Railtec transfers enable you to represent a fascinating range of styles and variations. Even in BR bauxite, there were a number of phases. The initial batches had BR-series numbers and plain, unlettered doors. Later they acquired UIC numbers and door brandings: at first 'Through to the Continent by British Railways' and the flying crate logo, later 'Through to the Continent by British Rail' with double-arrow symbol introduced in 1965. Grab handles were black originally, later white, while the arrow symbols on the end posts eventually disappeared.

FERRY VAN HISTORY CONTINUED...

BR official photograph of GB 787110, possibly taken at Ashford in 1963 immediately after construction. This early 'flying crate' livery was the one followed by Triang Hornby when its 4mm model was released in 1970 but by this date it was becoming rare on the prototype.

'British Railways' while others carried 'British Rail' branding; there was considerable variation in the bauxite-coloured plastic in which they were moulded. Because of the Continental associations there were also a number of vans in fictitious liveries – a Transfesa van in blue (R741), Interfrigo (R742) in white and Fyffe's Bananas in white and yellow (R786) without any lettering. There was also a dark blue version – now quite rare – with a Ford company logo (R787). None of these had any counterpart in real life.

Although several batches in authentic Railfreight livery were subsequently produced, the bauxite-liveried BR model was out of production for many years until it was reintroduced by Hornby (R6159) in 2002, by which time manufacturing had switched to China. The base model was much the same but the tampo-printed lettering was much better defined than on the Margate versions. The latest incarnations of this 47-year-old model were released in June 2017.

Intermediate
Beginner SKILL LEVEL Advanced

24

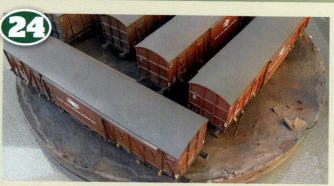

My weathering approach was, as so often, based around Lifecolor's invaluable 'Rail Weathering' and 'Black Rubber' sets. Here, prototypically, we have two vans in older liveries (as some were, right through to the late 1970s) alongside others carrying the then-new corporate branding.

25

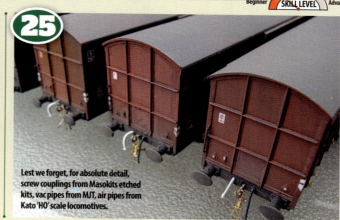

Lest we forget, for absolute detail, screw couplings from Masokits etched kits, vac pipes from MJT, air pipes from Kato 'HO' scale locomotives.

PART 3
10 OF A KIND

26 A parallel project was to create a complete train of ferry vans for *Hornby Magazine's* popular exhibition layout Twelve Trees Junction for its return to the show circuit in October and November 2017. With limited time at my disposal, I opted for a simplified approach that would deliver 80% of the result with 50% of the effort. In a layout context, overall effect often matters more than fine detail so I concentrated on lowering the axle units as before, shaving off the roof vents and reinstating the missing trusses – the modifications that I found made the biggest difference to my five super-detailed vans.

27

I felt I had to do something about the prominent tension-lock couplings, which are the same as those fitted to the original Triang-Hornby model of 1970. My solution was to fit the vans with an extended hook of 0.9mm brass wire at one end of the chassis, engaging with a D-shaped cut-out at the other. Soldering the hook to a brass 'staple' behind the buffer beam keeps everything square and stable.

28 The 2017 Hornby model represents a post-1973 TOPS-era ferry van (coded VIX) with replacement doors in a different colour. The BR logo is smaller than usual and the lettering is in a non-standard stencil style. I part-repainted and relettered all but one of the vans to create a much wider range of finishes, enhanced by strategic weathering. Once again Railtec transfers add the final touches with the 'Through to the Continent' branding and double-arrow symbol, this time in standard format. The new couplings are simple to use.

TIP

Building a block train of wagons like these, which will only ever run together in a fixed formation, bring its own small issues to contend with including vehicle order. So that these are always correctly set up on track each van is numbered.

Not long withdrawn from revenue service, B787289 still retained its red and grey Railfreight colours when stabled in the former goods yard at Huddersfield in April 1984. The overcast lighting reveals the subtle transverse lines where the roof panels have been welded together – they're not always visible in photographs. By this time the VIXs had received additional bracing on the ends.

Still very much in original condition apart from its Satlink livery and extra end bracing, KDB 786998 was in engineer's service when seen at Colchester in the early 1990s.

FUTURE PROOFING
YOUR LAYOUT

A model railway really can be for life if you build it with the right outlook from the start. **MIKE WILD** presents a selection of track plans for a modular layout system which can grow and develop with time.

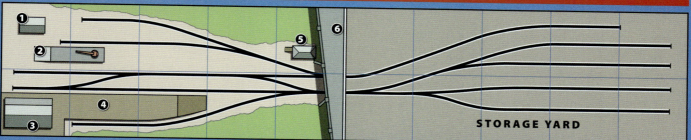

PLAN 1 SIMPLE TERMINUS, 10ft x 2ft.

STORAGE YARD

QUITE OFTEN what we want to build must be tempered by time, space, or money. We can't always go for the dream project straight away, but there are ways of making that happen – one of those being a modular design.

Modular layouts have been a common theme of national and online clubs – particularly overseas – where members build individual sections with set track spacing so that they can be joined together at events and meetings to create one big layout. But the concept of a modular model railway doesn't have to be kept for clubs. With the right design, a home layout can be built in a modular fashion, as we'll show here, allowing its construction to be staged as those important factors of time, space and money become available.

By starting with a simple branch line terminus, we can enhance the model over time to include a longer running line, more features and even to fill a whole room modelling more than one station. In fact, as you will see in our final version, with a little bit of redevelopment, the same basic station trackplan can even be taken on to create a continuous run double track main line.

A compelling case

So why would you build a modular style layout? Imagine that you currently have a two-bedroom home. There isn't a permanent space available for a model railway, but there are times at the weekend when you can take over a small area to assemble a layout. You don't want it to be too complicated at this point and, bearing in mind that it might only be up and running for a few hours at a time, it is important for your enjoyment that whatever you build can be set up in as little time as possible. You might only have a handful of items of rolling stock, but there is still plenty you can gain from the hobby even with these limitations. »

KEY
① **Store**
② **Loading dock**
③ **Station building**
④ **Platform**
⑤ **Signalbox**
⑥ **Road overbridge**

Developing a model railway can be done over time, as we have with Shortley Bridge. This layout is now 12ft x 12ft, but started off as a 10ft x 2ft terminus station. Most recently it has gained a second platform and new station buildings. Here a 'WD' 2-8-0 passes through with a mixed goods while a Clayton Type 1 waits for a clear path in the loop.
Mike Wild/Hornby Magazine.

TRACK PLANS

PLAN 2 EXTENDED TERMINUS, 12ft x 2ft.

STORAGE YARD

KEY

1. Store
2. Loading dock
3. Station building
4. Platform
5. Signalbox
6. Road
7. Headshunt
8. Factory
9. Backscene

Plan 1 shows a simple branch line terminus station which will fit on a single 5ft x 2ft baseboard. Connected to this is an additional 5ft baseboard to provide an area of off-scene storage. The layout can be separated into two sections for storage and once all the track is laid it would only take around 10-15 minutes to assemble. The 5ft x 2ft baseboard length is the maximum we would recommend for assembly by one person. Electrical connections can be as simple as a pair of plug-in terminal blocks to link the track feeds across the join. The track plan also shows both the main line and goods yard headshunt running off into the storage yard and there is good reason for this as you will see in Plan 2.

Plan 1 would all be built with medium radius points which would allow for anything up to medium sized tender engines – 0-6-0s, 4-4-0s and 2-6-0s – to be accommodated and only seven points are required to build the layout – four medium lefts and three medium rights.

Additional facilities are provided at the station beyond the main single platform with a secondary bay which could be used for a Diesel Multiple Unit (DMU), parcels van or even cattle traffic. The goods yard is modest, but the off-scene headshunt means that there will be plenty of opportunities for shunting pick-up goods trains to while away a Sunday afternoon. You could introduce a card system for goods trains, shuffling and dealing out four cards to select the vehicles which need to be formed into a train giving operation more direction.

The next level

However, while this simple track plan might be enough to keep you occupied initially, you might find that soon you have the time and

a little more space to work with allowing the layout to be expanded. Happily, this isn't too difficult.

The bridge which once formed the scenic break in Plan 1 would be removed carefully and repositioned a little further down the line to create a new scenic break. The original pair of 5ft long baseboards is extended with an extra 2ft x 2ft section taking the total length to 12ft – the typical length of a medium sized spare bedroom.

What we can do now is keep the station essentially the same, but introduce more operational features. The headshunt which was once hidden inside the storage yard is now fully scenic and the main line uses the original bridge, but in its new location, as the access to a redesigned storage yard. This has been kept compact to occupy 15in rather than the full 24in of the original plan leaving space in front to include a small rail-served factory site which is fed by an extra point set into the bay platform line. The addition of this single left-hand medium radius point expands the capacity and operational interest of the layout while the additional scenic section brings new modelling opportunities.

A permanent home

Time has moved on, the situation has changed and you now have a spare room or space in the garden for a shed to make the layout a permanent fixture. Until now, even in Plan 2, the layout might have had to remain portable to allow it to be packed away when not in use. With a dedicated space, your first thought might be to start from scratch, but there is no need as these next two plans will show.

First, in Plan 3, we've taken down the storage yard wall and added an 'L' shaped return to

the layout meaning that the original 12ft x 2ft section can now be fully scenic. The return adds a further 6ft to the track plan area and, while it doesn't add greatly to the scenic area, it does mean that more of that burgeoning rolling stock collection can be accommodated on track.

The factory site has also been modified – its connection being taken direct from the main line so that the line from the bay platform links into a single road engine shed. They are all small changes, but each one brings new modelling opportunities and more value from that initial plan which started off in Plan 1.

The next stage of development is to use the dedicated space for the layout to turn the 'L' into a 'U' shape. More stock space, a second station and a longer run for those wonderful locomotives are now all on the cards.

The original scenic area from Plan 3 remains unchanged in Plan 4, with the big adjustment being relocation of the storage yard. This 6ft long board can simply be disconnected from the 'L' shaped plan and moved around the room to its new location. The approach track might need adjusting to suit connection to the extended running line, but otherwise it stays »

A Clayton Type 1 ticks over in the station at Shortley Bridge.

PLAN 3 'L' SHAPED TERMINUS, 12ft x 8ft.

A simple road overbridge makes a perfect scenic break for the entry to a storage yard. Here a Sulzer Type 2 departs Shortley Bridge with a cement working.

KEY

1. Store
2. Loading dock
3. Station building
4. Platform
5. Signalbox
6. Water tower
7. Coal stage
8. Engine shed
9. Headshunt
10. Road bridge
11. Factory site
12. Backscene
13. Traverser storage yard – note, this could be a conventional pointed storage yard or a cassette yard depending upon how you wish to operate the layout.

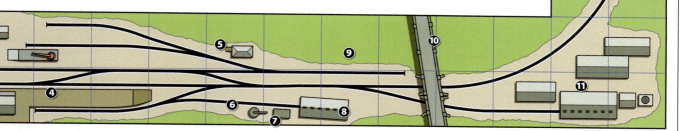

PLAN 4 'U' SHAPED TERMINUS, 12ft x 8ft.

STORAGE YARD

KEY

1. Store	11. Factory
2. Loading dock	12. Level crossing
3. Station building	13. Crossing keeper's cottage
4. Platform	14. Farm house
5. Signalbox	15. Coal staithes
6. Water column	16. Store
7. Coal stage	17. Halt
8. Engine shed	18. Approach road
9. Headshunt	19. Backscene
10. Road overbridge	20. Traverser

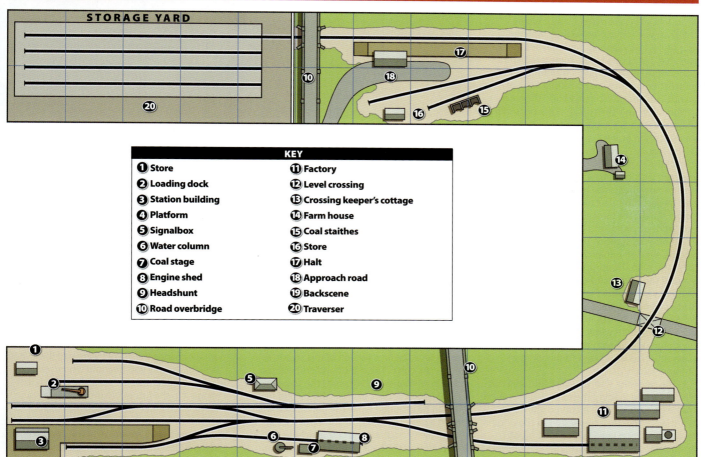

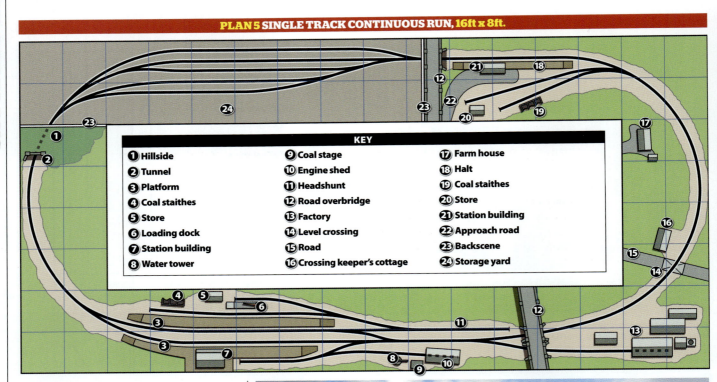

PLAN 5 SINGLE TRACK CONTINUOUS RUN, 16ft x 8ft.

KEY

❶ Hillside	❾ Coal stage	⓱ Farm house
❷ Tunnel	❿ Engine shed	⓲ Halt
❸ Platform	⓫ Headshunt	⓳ Coal staithes
❹ Coal staithes	⓬ Road overbridge	⓴ Store
❺ Store	⓭ Factory	㉑ Station building
❻ Loading dock	⓮ Level crossing	㉒ Approach road
❼ Station building	⓯ Road	㉓ Backscene
❽ Water tower	⓰ Crossing keeper's cottage	㉔ Storage yard

the same.

The longer running line means we can add more scenic features – a farm or cottage scene maybe - overlooking the railway, while we can also add a small halt on the approach to the storage yard with a road passing above the railway to form the scenic break. It's all going well and each time the layout is enhanced it develops a more realistic picture of a working branch line.

A continuous run

Most modellers yearn for a layout where they can sit back and enjoy their locomotives operating, but with a terminus layout that isn't possible. Trains need to be monitored and controlled – no bad thing – throughout their journey, but what if we could make the existing layout into one which ran around the room?

With a few adjustments that is a possibility, although Plan 5 is more of a rebuild than an expansion as it will require adjustment of the storage yard position, potentially the loss of the second station, and expansion of the layout's length by 4ft. In total, the whole design now measures 16ft x 8ft – a size which can be accommodated in a typical 16ft x 8ft single garage, or maybe that new timber shed you've been promising yourself!

The original station, goods facility and engine shed all remain from Plans 3 and 4 together with the lengthened scenic run around the right-hand corner. The longer storage yard means that even more of your stock can be out and ready to run plus, if you felt the need, you could introduce a cassette connection point allowing further trains to be stored underneath the layout for quick connection to a dedicated siding in the storage yard.

At the opposite end, a new scenic area can be developed leading the railway back round to the original station. A curved left-hand point will make the connection to the original terminus station lines, with a little bit of additional scenic modelling being required to blend the ballasting and extend the platforms

Bringing a small goods yard to life is simple with readily available accessories.

to have new ramps at the left hand end.

It's an impressive layout now with plenty of potential. A train can be left to circulate or you can take full control for a detailed operating session – the only limitation now is the single track main line. Two trains running on a double track would be the pinnacle for this development.

Double track

Can it be done? Yes, although there will be a greater requirement for modification of the scenery to accommodate a double-track main line into Plan 5. We could prepare for this by including the double track around the left-hand end in the development of Plan 5 which would save considerable upheaval to achieve the final version of this layout, as drawn in Plan 6. The right-hand end will see the most intensive changes as the scenery will need to be cut back to allow the second main line to be included while the goods yard will need a new headshunt. If you were feeling particularly creative, you could include a goods loop around the back of the inner platform, expanding the capacity of the station further.

Also noteworthy is that the factory and single road engine shed have now gone. They have made way for a larger locomotive facility including a double track engine shed, coal road and water tower. There isn't quite enough space for a turntable here – as nice as it would be – so locomotives requiring turning will need to be handled off-scene.

The result after all those years of modelling and acquisition of space is a railway to enjoy and operate for years to come. Scenic development will take time and even though you have reached what we are calling completion, there is still room for further detailing, finishing and enhancement. New buildings might become available, you may want to try your hand at scratchbuilding to create a unique structure or perhaps change the era or location of the layout.

Whichever way you turn and whatever you build there will always be the chance to change it in the future. No model railway is ever finished and even though Plan 6 is our conclusion for this feature, we hope you will be able to see the journey this railway has taken to get here. Design, build, enjoy – that's what the hobby's all about! ∎

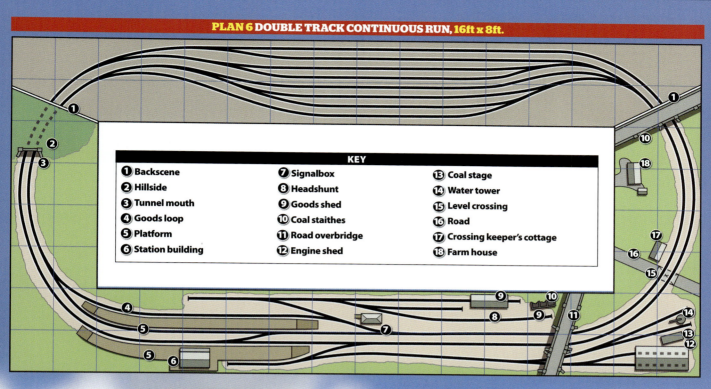

PLAN 6 DOUBLE TRACK CONTINUOUS RUN, 16ft x 8ft.

KEY

❶ Backscene	❼ Signalbox	⓭ Coal stage
❷ Hillside	❽ Headshunt	⓮ Water tower
❸ Tunnel mouth	❾ Goods shed	⓯ Level crossing
❹ Goods loop	❿ Coal staithes	⓰ Road
❺ Platform	⓫ Road overbridge	⓱ Crossing keeper's cottage
❻ Station building	⓬ Engine shed	⓲ Farm house

A Peppercorn 'K1' 2-6-0 crosses the road bridge on the approach to Felton Cement Works.

BRITISH 'Pacifics'

For more than a century, the 'Pacific' has represented the pinnacle of design achievement for British steam, producing some of the fastest and most powerful locomotives ever to run in this country. **EVAN GREEN-HUGHES** finds out why this wheel arrangement came to be so dominant.

TRAVEL BY STEAM TRAIN arguably reached its glamorous peak between the two world wars during the first half of the 20th century. Four major independent companies vied with each other for passenger numbers, and in the process transformed rail travel into the epitome of luxury – for First Class passengers at least. Services were introduced with facilities such as on-board hairdressing, fine dining and luxury seating, and these were promoted widely with innovative poster and advertising campaigns. The public became enthralled with the railways, with particular interest being shown in the racing image which the publicists portrayed, an image that centred round a series of fast and powerful locomotives, most of which were of the 'Pacific' - 4-6-2 - wheel arrangement.

Peppercorn 'A1' 60131 *Osprey* makes a spirited run through Hawick with a Millerhill-Leeds fitted freight routed via the Waverley route to Carlisle on July 29 1964. These machines were equally at home on freight as well as passenger work. *Norman Preedy Archive/Railphotoprints.co.uk.*

The rivalry was most fierce between the London Midland & Scottish Railway (LMS) and the London and North Eastern Railway (LNER), which had competing routes from London to Scotland and this resulted in a series of high-speed trials which eventually led to 'A4' 4-6-2 4468 *Mallard* being officially recognised as the fastest steam locomotive in the world. Its speed record of 126mph, achieved on July 3 1938, remains to this day. The A4's competitor, the 'Princess Coronation' class, achieved only 114mph but was arguably the most powerful engine of the two and might have held the crown had the LMS possessed a suitable piece of high-speed track on which to make a record attempt.

So great was the public's interest in these races and in the railways of the period that even today there are few people who have not heard of the exploits of *Mallard* while 'Pacifics' of all types remain one of the most popular types of steam locomotive active on our heritage railways and also on the national network.

Air-smoothed 'Battle of Britain' 4-6-2 34071 *601 Squadron* hurries through Bromley at the head of the down 'Golden Arrow' in 1955. *Railphotoprints.co.uk.*

American origins

So what is a 'Pacific' - and why did the design prove to be so popular in the heady days of steam? All locomotives built to this style have six driving wheels mounted on three axles and these provide all the traction to drive the train along. So that fast running can be achieved, the driving wheels are usually of quite large diameter and the design is arranged so that these wheels take most of the weight of the engine, assisting with adhesion. At the front is a two axle four-wheel bogie and at the rear a single axle which allows a wide firebox to be supported.

It is not absolutely clear where the name 'Pacific' comes from but it is most likely from the Missouri Pacific Railroad in the USA, which was the first railway to use the type on that continent in 1902. Its locomotives were logical enlargements of the then popular 4-4-2s and followed on from a batch of similar engines built by the Baldwin Locomotive Works in Philadelphia the previous year for the New Zealand Railways.

Baldwin had developed the type in response to a request for a locomotive that could burn poor quality coal and which required a much larger firebox than was the custom at that time. It was quickly realised that not only did the rear pony truck allow for the larger firebox but it also dampened out any tendency the engine had to sway from side to side and aided running at speed. Large numbers were soon under construction for Australia, the United States, Canada and New Zealand with the popularity of the type spreading as far as South Africa by 1903. Despite the 'Pacifics' increasing popularity abroad, it wasn't until 1908 that the class first made an appearance in the United Kingdom. Here the 4-4-2 and the 4-4-0 were still the predominant types used for express work but the increasing popularity of rail travel was leading to the use of heavier and longer trains and there was also a demand for greater speeds, both of which meant that more powerful locomotives would have to be designed.

Rather surprisingly it was the Great Western Railway that was to be the first in the UK to construct a 'Pacific' – even though its 'Saint' and 'Star' 4-6-0s were by some measure the best express passenger locomotives in the country. In 1908 the railway's Chief Mechanical Engineer George Jackson Churchward was looking at ways of providing engines larger than the 'Star' 4-6-0s which were used on the heaviest and fastest trains of the era. He concluded that a much larger boiler would be needed and to prove his theories he worked out a new design which had an enormous barrel 23ft long. Because of its size, this boiler required a large firebox, some 20% bigger than the 'Stars' and this could only be accommodated if a pair of trailing wheels was added to the normal GWR 4-6-0 configuration.

The locomotive that resulted was numbered 111 and received the name *The Great Bear* and when it was built it was the largest locomotive in the country, something which was of great value to the railway's publicity department. Unfortunately the engine wasn't a great success, probably because the front end design was copied directly from the earlier engines and its high axle loading led to it having restricted route availability. The Great Western didn't build any more 'Pacifics' because it was found that by using good quality Welsh coal, sufficient thermal efficiency could be obtained from a narrower firebox, which could then be conveniently sited between a locomotive's rear driving wheels.

A further 14 years were to elapse before the design once again made an appearance on Britain's railways. In 1922 the Great Northern Railway (GNR) was operating its crack East Coast Main Line (ECML) expresses with Ivatt's large-boilered 4-4-2s but these were struggling to cope with the demands placed on them by the operating department, both in respect of speed and haulage ability. As a result, double-heading often had to be used but that was expensive in terms of machinery and men. Nigel Gresley had become Chief Mechanical Engineer of the GNR in 1911 and within a few years he had begun to draw out an enlarged version of the Ivatt engine which would have had four cylinders. However, such a locomotive would not have had the necessary boiler capacity and therefore it proved necessary to think again, with attention then falling on the 'Pacific' wheel arrangement.

The BR 'Clan' class was small and not widely successful when compared with the larger 'Britannias'. On June 30 1963 'Clan' 72006 *Clan Mackenzie* is about to leave Carlisle Citadel with the 1.05pm Manchester-Glasgow service while Stanier 'Duchess' 46249 *City of Sheffield* waits in the centre to relieve the northbound 'Royal Scot'. *Hugh Ballantyne/Railphotoprints.co.uk.*

In its pre-preservation days rebuilt 'Merchant Navy' 35028 *Clan Line* brews up prior to departure from Waterloo with a down Bournemouth service in 1964. In their rebuilt form the 'Merchants' were highly capable locomotives which regularly achieved 100mph running even in their final weeks of service. *Railphotoprints.co.uk.*

The new breed

What emerged from Doncaster was radically different from what had gone before. Gresley's new engines were built to the extremities of the loading gauge, with a wide boiler and huge firebox which extended downwards almost as far as the pair of trailing wheels. To cope with all the steam that the boiler could produce, three cylinders were provided in a style which was to become much more familiar over the next few years.

There were also several revolutionary features of the lower part of the engine with both the front and rear bogies being ingeniously designed to cope with sharp curves as well as fast running on straight tracks. First out of the shops was 1470 *Great Northern* and this was soon followed by 1471 which initially ran around without a name. Co-incidentally further north one of the GNR's partners in the ECML, the North Eastern Railway, was also being provided with a 'Pacific', and for similar reasons. In this case, designer Vincent Raven produced something which was not quite so radical as Gresley's engine, being in essence an

The mighty Stanier 'Duchess' 4-6-2s had the title of the most powerful 'Pacifics' on the British railway network with recordings of 3,300hp at the cylinders. On March 25 1964 46238 *City of Carlisle* waits impatiently at Preston as it heads a northbound express. *Paul Claxton/Railphotoprints.co.uk.*

Leeds Holbeck's Gresley 'A3' 60038 *Firdaussi* leaves Leeds City in 1961 displaying its double chimney. *Jim Carter/Railphotoprints.co.uk.*

enlarged version of the 'C7' 4-4-2 with a bigger boiler and firebox as well as an extra axle. After the two companies were amalgamated into the LNER in 1923 trials were held to see which of the two was the best and in the event the 'A1', as Gresley's engines had become, came out the best and were selected for further development.

Over the next decade or so the basic design laid out by Gresley in 1922 continued to be developed and refined. The 'A1s' gained higher pressure boilers and better valves to eventually become reclassified as 'A3s' with which we are all familiar today and in this form they were easily capable of handling the heaviest and fastest trains that were contained within the LNER's timetable. One of these engines was the famous 1472 (later 4472) *Flying Scotsman* itself, a locomotive that was to achieve a number of records for steam traction, being the first to be officially recognised as having achieved a speed of 100mph and also setting new standards for non-stop runs between London and Scotland.

The streamlined 'A4' which followed in 1935 is to many the most beautiful steam engine that has ever been designed. A total of 35 of these three-cylinder racehorses were built. The high speeds with this design were achieved by applying internal streamlining to the steam passages, raising the boiler pressure and extending the firebox and later by fitting a double chimney and Kylchap exhaust, which assisted with drawing air through the fire. Outwardly the 'A4s' were noted for their streamlined design which was partly there to smooth the passage of the train through the air, partly to aid in lifting the smoke away from the front of the engine and largely because of the publicity value that ensued as the public admired the modern and futuristic looking engines.

The ultimate?

Of course Nigel Gresley didn't have it all his own way for, over on the LMS, William Stanier was also moving into 'Pacific' power for his company's crack expresses. Design work there started in the mid-1920s when there was a desire from the traffic department for trains running longer distances on the West Coast Main Line but it really got underway when Stanier arrived from the Great Western.

In construction and detail what were to become the 'Princess Royals' set completely new standards for the LMS, with much of the locomotive based on Swindon practice and incorporating a large taper boiler with four-cylinder drive. Two conventional locomotives were built and put to work hauling trains such as the 'Royal Scot' between London and Glasgow whilst a third was built with turbine drive as an experiment to see if better power could be obtained by this alternative method. A series of trials held in 1936 proved the feasibility of reducing timings so that they could directly compete with the LNER, but non-stop running proved not to be possible because space could not be spared in the tender for the corridor required for crew changes due to the critical

> *"The 'Princess Royals' set new standards for LMS locomotives."*
>
> **EVAN GREEN-HUGHES**

amount of coal needed for the journey.

By this time 12 'Princess Royals' had been built and the new accelerated timings required more engines but rather than build more of what they already had the LMS went for a larger and improved version, which was to become known as the 'Princess Coronation' class.

These engines were true rivals for the LNER both in terms of raw power and also looks, for Stanier had sanctioned some of them to be constructed with streamlined casings painted in a livery to match the new streamlined stock but there was one prize that both companies wanted, that of fastest steam engine in the world. In 1937 6220 *Coronation* achieved 114mph, but in the process took a set of points at Crewe rather faster than intended, putting an end to any more high speed attempts. Almost a year later *Mallard* was to smash that record but by this time it had been generally recognised that the 'Princess Coronation' was the most powerful of the two, achieving more than 2,000hp whilst under test over Shap, and estimations of around 3,300hp being developed in the cylinders, making them more powerful than any other WCML locomotives until the advent of the electrics in the 1960s.

The Second World War put an end to the racing and all the British 'Pacifics' were turned to slower, but very heavy, trains. The government would not allow companies to build any more express engines during the hostilities but even so Oliver Bulleid of the Southern Railway managed to wangle the construction of two designs, the 'Merchant Navy' and the lighter 'West Country'/'Battle of Britain' towards the end of the conflict. This was on the grounds that they were really mixed traffic engines, a move which must have fooled someone as 110 were eventually built.

Both contained a number of radical features. There was much more welding involved than previously, which speeded up production; a number of weight-saving measures had been incorporated; pressed wheels were fitted as was

The experimental 'Turbomotive' Stanier 'Princess Royal' 46202 climbs away from Halton Junction with the 5.25am Liverpool Lime Street-Euston on May 21 1949. This 2,400hp 'Princess' was rebuilt in conventional form in 1952 with new cylinders and frames and was named *Princess Anne*, but two months later it was destroyed in the 1952 Harrow and Wealdstone disaster. *R A Whitfield/Railphotoprints.co.uk.*

encased chain-driven valve gear. The public saw only the 'air smoothed' casings which gave these locomotives a unique appearance, which once again proved to be a gift to the publicists. Although very competent engines, they proved quite difficult to handle, with slipping at the start of a journey being a particular problem. They were, however, brilliant steamers and most lasted well into the 1960s – and some to the very last day of steam on the Southern Region, although many were rebuilt in more conventional form without the air smoothed casings and with conventional valve gear.

Last of the breed

Back on the Eastern Region, Darlington Works also turned out its 'A2s' to the design of Edward Thompson in 1944. These were of mixed traffic design, too, but unlike Bulleid's engines proved to be under-boilered and lacking in adhesion. Construction carried on for a couple of years but when Thompson retired his successor, Arthur Peppercorn, cancelled the rest, instead preferring to produce his own version, which was to become the mixed traffic 'A2' and the 'A1', which was the company's new standard express engine. Advanced features such as self-cleaning smokeboxes, electric lights and roller bearings made these machines truly the highest of engineering achievement for their time, but there was little need for such powerful engines in post-war years and much of the time both classes were worked far short of their actual capacity.

When British Railways was nationalised in 1948 it was quickly decided that a fleet of standard steam engines would be produced but until the design was finalised construction

of some of the existing 'Pacifics' was continued. The largest number were of the LNER's new Peppercorn 'A1' class, with 49 of these being built, along with 14 of the smaller-wheeled 'A2s' but the Southern Region was also able to add 40 more 'West Countries' and another 10 'Merchant Navys'. The Midland added just one 'Princess Coronation' to its stud.

While this was going on plans were being finalised for the standard fleet. Bulleid and Peppercorn had shown the advantages of free-running mixed traffic 'Pacifics' and therefore a scheme was proposed for a locomotive with 6ft 2in driving wheels that was soon to become universally known as the 'Britannia' – the first

two-cylinder 4-6-2s to run in Britain.

Three batches, totalling 55 engines, were built with the design best described as of LMS heritage by way of Southern influence with an emphasis on up-to-date technology and ease of operation. A number of weight reduction measures were also incorporated into the design in an effort to improve route availability. The first batch of locomotives got off to a bad start when there were complaints that the driving wheels were shifting on their axles and there were also complaints from the passengers about a fore-and-aft motion. Despite these issues the crews were very enthusiastic about the engines, and

> *"Construction of existing 'Pacifics' continued under BR"*
>
> **EVAN GREEN-HUGHES**

BRITISH RAILWAYS OPERATED 4-6-2s			
Class	**Designer**	**Builder**	**Total built**
'Merchant Navy' 4-6-2	Oliver Bulleid	SR/BR	30
'West Country'/'Battle of Britain' 4-6-2	Oliver Bulleid	SR/BR	110
'Princess Royal 4-6-2	William Stanier	LMS	12
'Princess Coronation' 4-6-2	William Stanier	LMS/BR	38
'A1' 4-6-2	Arthur Peppercorn	LNER/BR	49
'A1/1' 4-6-2	Edward Thompson	LNER	1
'A2'	Arthur Peppercorn	LNER/BR	15
'A2/1' 4-6-2	Edward Thompson	LNER	4
'A2/2' 4-6-2	Edward Thompson	LNER	6
'A2/3' 4-6-2	Edward Thompson	LNER	15
'A3' 4-6-2	Nigel Gresley	LNER	78
'A4' 4-6-2	Nigel Gresley	LNER	35
'Britannia' 4-6-2	Robert Riddles	BR	55
'Clan' 4-6-2	Robert Riddles	BR	10
'Duke' 4-6-2	Robert Riddles	BR	1

'Britannia' class 'Pacific' 70004
William Shakespeare makes
a dramatic departure from
Penrith with a southbound
service on July 22 1967.
Chris Davies/Railphotoprints.co.uk

The Gresley 'A4s' were instantly recognisable and even in later form without valances their streamlined casing set them apart from everything else. In 1957 60032 *Gannet* rumbles onto the swing bridge at Selby as it heads a northbound East Coast Main Line service. *Railphotoprints.co.uk.*

in particular about the cabs that had been designed to be as comfortable as possible, with a convenient layout of controls, and which were mounted on the boiler, rather than the frames so as to reduce vibration. As with previous Pacifics these engines were a delight to the public relations people, as their high-stepping footplating gave them a modern and dynamic appearance.

Although the 'Britannias' had a wide route availability there were still some lines, particularly in Scotland, on which they could not be used. A lighter version, with smaller cylinders and boiler, was therefore drawn up and ten were constructed, becoming known as the 'Clan' class. These locomotives were never as successful as the 'Britannia', having a reputation for poor steaming and any plans for further examples were killed off when the 1955 Modernisation Plan was announced. Built in 1951 and 1952 these engines were to have a very short life, with the first batch being taken out of service in 1962 and with the class being extinct four years later.

British Railways did have a third design of 'Pacific', although in the event only one example was ever constructed. 71000 *Duke of Gloucester* was a high-powered machine which was almost never built because in the early 1950s BR had sufficient locomotives for its needs. However a tragic accident at Harrow and Wealdstone in 1952 led to the loss of one of the 'Princess Royals' and the opportunity was then taken to build what was intended to be a prototype of a new class. The 'Duke' was completed in 1954 and was in fact an enlarged version of the 'Britannia' with three cylinders instead of two and was equipped with the latest style of Caprotti rotary valve gear. Unfortunately, mistakes made in the design meant that this locomotive never achieved what was hoped of it and any further development was then killed off when the decision was taken to switch to diesel traction. The engine was taken out of service in 1962 when only ten years old and at first was intended for the National Collection. Instead,

> ### "Amazingly, in 2008 a brand new Peppercorn 'A1' was built."
> **EVAN GREEN-HUGHES**

only one set of valve gear was preserved and 71000 went off to Woodham's scrapyard in Wales from where it was rescued in 1974 and, after a lot of effort and pioneering work, returned to working order. Ironically, during the restoration process the faults with the original design were recognised and corrected with the result that the locomotive became one of the most powerful ever to work on the main line.

But there was more to come, because amazingly, in 2008, a brand-new Peppercorn 'A1' was built thanks to a massive fundraising and engineering effort. Not only was it for a time the newest locomotive of any type in the country, in 2017 it became the first steam locomotive in Britain for 50 years to officially break the 100mph mark as part of tests to allow it to run at 90mph on charter trains – an outstanding achievement for steam in the 21st century.

The term 'Pacific' is usually used to refer to tender engines with the 4-6-2 wheel arrangement but there were also six different tank engine examples put into service in the UK. The London & North Western Railway had the 'Prince of Wales' type for suburban duties, the North Eastern had the 'Ys' (later 'A7') for freight train work, the London Brighton & South Coast had the solitary 'J1' for express passenger work, the London & South Western had the 'H16', the Great Central had its hugely successful 'A5' while in Scotland the Caledonian had the '944' for suburban work. Although these shared the wheel arrangement of their larger, tender equipped cousins, their development was largely to accommodate more coal and water capacity and as such they are not really part of the main 'Pacific' story.

From 1908 to the present day, the 'Pacifics' of the railways of Britain have represented the ultimate in steam locomotive design and in the process captured the imagination of engineers and the public alike in a way that had never been achieved before. They were amongst the most powerful locomotives ever built and were undoubtedly the fastest, and in many ways they did much to pave the way for the high-speed railway that we have today. ■

The Gresley 'A4' 4-6-2 4467 *Wild Swan* leaves Gas Works tunnel as it heads out of London King's Cross with the down 'Coronation' in July 1938 – a stunning example of the glamorous era of 1930s rail travel. *Rail Archive Stephenson.*

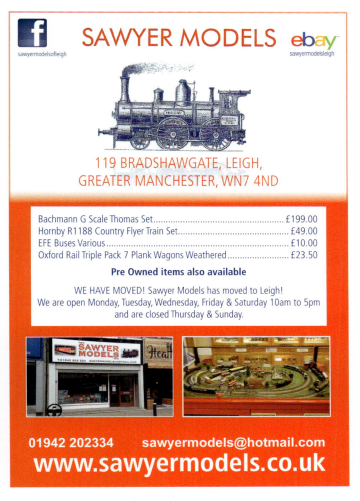

Working class
HEROES

More and more models of small shunting locomotives are reaching our shops, giving us plenty of choice for station pilots, goods yards and industrial sidings. **BEN JONES** looks at what is available and what's coming soon.

EVER SINCE model railways were first invented, big express passenger locomotives with their fancy liveries and polished nameplates have stolen the limelight. Goods engines and shunting types - the machines that did all the real work - earning their living out of the public eye, have always had a much lower profile. Until now ready-to-run manufacturers have largely exhausted the pool of large express passenger locomotives, mixed traffic and middleweight types. Even the humble 0-6-0 tender goods type has appeared in many forms over the last few years. As companies search for their next projects, they are increasingly looking to the smaller end of the locomotive fleet for inspiration. The result of this is an increasingly good selection of

steam tank locomotives and diesel shunters, both from main line companies and the world of industrials. After years of neglect, the latter category is suddenly in vogue with manufacturers, and new models are appearing in 'OO' and 'O' gauges in particular.

Shunting and small goods locomotives were a remarkably diverse bunch as each company built or bought its own designs suited to particular purposes. Even in BR diesel days, a policy of awarding contracts to a wide range of suppliers resulted in dozens of different designs - not always with great success - some of which only lasted a few years. What follows is a survey of what is currently available from ready-to-run manufacturers in 'OO' gauge, plus a brief look at the situation in 'N' and 'O' gauge and a spot of 'crystal ball gazing' to assess where the gaps are and what might come next.

'Big Four' steam

We start with the Great Western Railway (GWR), which was dominated by the various designs of 0-6-0 'Pannier' tank. Most of these were designed for specific goods or passenger duties so don't fall into this survey, but the ubiquitous '57XX'/'8750' general purpose warrants a mention as many were employed on yard shunting and station pilot duties until the 1960s. Bachmann can supply both the original cab '57XX' and later welded style cab '8750' version. It will also add the larger post-war '94XX' type in 2018.

Two smaller GWR outside-cylinder 0-6-0Ts are the subject of new and forthcoming OO models by two different manufacturers. Both Kernow Model Rail Centre/DJ Models and Heljan have developed models of the little '1361' 0-6-0ST, which can trace its origins back to the Cornwall »

A Heljan 'OO' gauge Class 05 shunts at Felton Cement Works alongside a Hornby Class 08. These two shunters represent just a small selection of the available range of diesel motive power for 'OO' yard work.

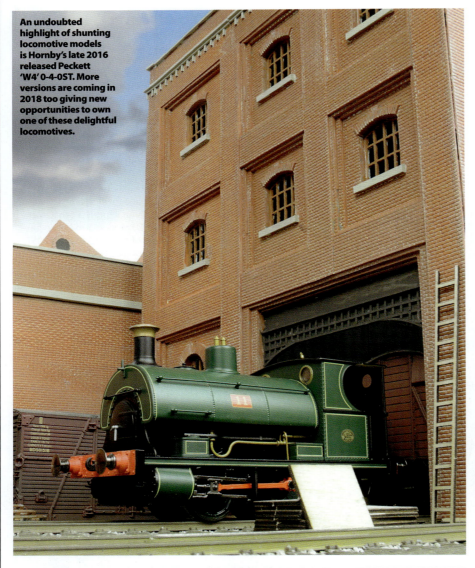

An undoubted highlight of shunting locomotive models is Hornby's late 2016 released Peckett 'W4' 0-4-0ST. More versions are coming in 2018 too giving new opportunities to own one of these delightful locomotives.

Hornby's 'OO' gauge Sentinel 4wDH arrived in 2014 representing the manufacturer's return to industrial locomotive models. It is available in 4w and 0-4-0 formats in a range of liveries.

Minerals Railway in 1874, but updated and 'Swindonised' by Churchward/Holcroft in 1910, and the later '1366' 0-6-0PT, introduced in 1934. Both were built for shunting docks and other locations where locomotive size and wheelbase was limited by sharp curves and tight clearances. Heljan's model is already available and KMRC's is due to follow in late-2017. With just five and six locomotives built respectively, the availability of two competing 'OO' models is remarkable. At the beginners' end of the market, Hornby has its long-standing model of one-off GWR 0-4-0T No. 101, which is available in the Railroad budget range.

Moving on to the Southern Railway/Region, the options have improved considerably in the last couple of years. Dapol is well advanced with a new model of the tiny LSWR Adams 'B4' 0-4-0T dock shunter for release in late-2017/early-2018. It will join the superb Bachmann 'USA' dock tank, which is available now in a wide range of SR, BR, military and industrial liveries. These chunky 0-6-0Ts were built in the USA and shipped to Europe to support the D-Day invasion force, later going on to see use with the SR and right across Europe and Asia.

For something a little more dainty, Kernow Model Rail Centre has its lovely Beattie '0298' 2-4-0WT, as used on the Wenford Bridge branch in Cornwall from the late-19th century until 1962. Several versions are available with detail variations across the final Wadebridge-based trio.

Not strictly a shunting locomotive, but certainly

at the smaller end of the fleet is Hornby's LBSCR Stroudley 'Terrier' 0-6-0T. This ex-Dapol model has been around for a long time and would benefit from re-tooling to modern standards in the future.

The latest plan for a Southern shunting engine is Hatton's August 2017 announcement of the South Eastern and Chatham Railway 'P' 0-6-0T which is expected to be released in 12 different liveries in December 2017-January 2018. These attractive and compact 0-6-0Ts are sure to be popular, not least for their ornate early pre-grouping liveries.

Over on Midland lines, Bachmann's Johnson '1F' 0-6-0T is one of the company's best OO models and a classic late-Victorian shunting locomotive. Both half-cab and full cab versions are available in LMS and BR liveries. Bachmann also offers the half-cab's bigger sister, in the form of a Fowler 3F 'Jinty' 0-6-0T. Although it hasn't been in the range for some years, Hornby has the charming ex-Dapol model of the Lancashire & Yorkshire Railway (LYR) 'Pug' 0-4-0ST in its fleet – for many years the smallest 'OO' gauge locomotive you could buy.

Hornby's other 'Pug' is a Railroad product, best known to most people as 'Smokey Joe'. This is based on a Caledonian Railway design used in Scotland. At just over £30 it's ideal for kids with its hypersonic speed but not so good for shunting because of that.

Of the 'Big Four' companies, the London and North Eastern Railway (LNER) is perhaps best furnished with good models of shunting locomotives. Smallest is the Dapol Sentinel 4w vertical boiler tank (a special commission), which is available in many versions covering single speed 'Y1' and twin speed 'Y3' sub-classes, plus London Midland & Scottish Railway (LMS), GWR and industrial variants. Rapido Trains has been commissioned to produce the LNER 'J70' 0-6-0T tram engine, most famously used on the Wisbech & Upwell Tramway and immortalised by Rev. W Awdry as 'Toby' in the 'Thomas the Tank Engine' stories.

Hornby and DJ Models both offer models of the Hunslet 'Austerity' 0-6-0ST, some of which were sold to the LNER and became 'J94s'. DJM's model of 2016 is more detailed, with numerous detail variations, than the Hornby product, which dates back to Dapol in the 1980s.

Hornby also has a trio of larger LNER 0-6-0T shunting locomotives, the North British Railway 'J83', Great Northern 'J52' and its most recent the LNER 'J50'. The latter Gresley design, with its distinctive sloping side tanks, is by far the best of the bunch, having been released for the first time in 2016. The very basic 'J83' and elderly 'J52' are now obsolete, with no DCC provision, and may only appear again in train sets.

Finally, the prize for longevity goes to Bachmann for its North Eastern Railway/LNER 'J72' 0-6-0T. First introduced by Mainline in 1976, it was resurrected and given a new chassis in the 1990s and will finally be retired and replaced by an all-new model in 2018.

Industrial interlude

Until very recently, anyone wanting to model industrial operations had to rely on re-liveried ex-main line locomotives, of which there have been many over the years, or turn to the many kit products on the market. However, there's now an increasing selection of good quality models of purely industrial locomotives, both steam and diesel.

First of the new generation to appear in 'OO' was Hornby's Sentinel 4w diesel, which is offered in a wide range of liveries, with or without outside cranks. The success of that little diesel led Hornby to introduce a tiny steam industrial too, in the gorgeous form of the Peckett 'W4' 0-4-0ST. These proved to be extremely popular and sold out quickly, but more batches are due in 2018. I wouldn't be surprised to see more industrial locomotives from this source over the next couple of years. DCC users should be aware that both the Sentinel and Peckett models need a Hornby X9659 four-pin decoder.

More rudimentary are the Hornby Railroad Bagnall 0-4-0 diesel, which shares a chassis with the GWR No. 101, 'Smokey Joe', BR Class 06 (see below) and two freelance industrial 0-4-0Ts often seen in basic train sets.

Altogether more detailed is the DJ Models Hunslet 'Austerity', which is offered in numerous short-run batches covering many different industrial, War Department and LNER/BR liveries, with many prototypical detail variations to items such as cabs, chimneys and footsteps. DJM also »

Bachmann's Fowler '1F' 0-6-0T has been released in 'OO' in both half and full cab versions. Behind stands a Bachmann Class 08 in original BR black with early crests.

On the left is the Dapol produced 'OO' Sentinel 'Y3' 4wVBT, a commissioned model, alongside the much larger Hornby 'J50' 0-6-0T. Both have shunting pedigree, but offer substantially different appearances.

promised a 'OO' gauge version of the Hudswell, Clarke 'Countess of Warwick' 0-6-0ST a couple of years ago, although no tangible evidence of it has yet been presented.

The most recent addition to the industrial ranks is Golden Valley Hobbies' Yorkshire Engine Co. 'Janus' 0-6-0 diesel shunter, designed and produced by Oxford Rail. Offered in British Steel, NCB, BP and Port of London liveries, with or without DCC sound, it's an impressive representative of the 1950s/60s generation of British industrial diesels.

The most recent announcement for industrial modellers comes from Hatton's which is producing its own exclusive model of the Andrew Barclay 14in and 16in 0-4-0ST for 'OO' gauge. This all-new product is set for release at the end of January 2018 following its announcement in August 2017 and will make a great stablemate for the Hornby Peckett 0-4-0ST.

Recent successes in this area virtually guarantee that more ready-to-run 'OO' gauge industrials will appear over the next few years, it's just a matter of who chooses what. Look out though for more small 0-6-0T steam types and possibly a new diesel or two. Before we move on to BR diesel shunters, don't forget that many of these also moved on to industrial use after withdrawal by BR – some when they were just a few years old. Bachmann, Hornby and Heljan have produced, or are planning, versions of their Class 03, 04, 05, 07 and 08/09 models in post-BR industrial guise.

Diesel diversity

The LMS pioneered diesel traction for shunting duties in the 1920s and 1930s, providing the basis for more widespread dieselisation by BR in the 1950s. While none of the early pre-1945 types are available in ready-to-run form, many of their descendants are.

Bachmann's diesel range includes an excellent BR 204hp 0-6-0DM, better known as Class 03, which covers various detail changes seen on the class, including later dual-braked locomotives and industrial examples. The similar but older Drewry Class 04 is currently being revamped and will next appear with a new DCC-ready chassis. Bachmann also offers a BR/English Electric 350hp 0-6-0DE Class 08/09 in a wide range of liveries and with many detail variations according to livery and batch.

However, that '08/09' is bettered by Hornby's superb model which offers finer detail and a DCC sound option, as well as opening cab doors and finely produced radiator slats. If your budget doesn't stretch to that, Hornby RailRoad can furnish you with a basic Class 08 sitting on a generic inside frame 0-6-0 steam locomotive chassis. The RailRoad range also features a much rarer BR diesel type, an Andrew Barclay Class 06 204hp 0-4-0DM. The proportions of this Scottish shunter have been significantly distorted to accommodate the basic Hornby 0-4-0 chassis.

Heljan is a more recent entrant into the diesel shunter field, but has added a couple of welcome alternatives to the BR standard designs. First to arrive was the Hunslet Class 05 204hp 0-6-0DM, in its later guise with larger cab and panoramic windows and larger diameter wheels. This very nice model is available in BR, preserved and industrial liveries and will soon be joined by a Ruston Hornsby Class 07 0-6-0DE. Just 14 of these attractive locomotives with offset centre cabs were built to replace the 'USA' tanks shunting Southampton Docks. However, they were soon rendered redundant and some went into industrial service. Heljan's model will cover both BR and industrial versions.

Possibilities

Looking at the list above, what stands out is the absence of a good quality small BR 0-4-0 diesel, such as the Yorkshire Engine Class 02. Numerous 0-4-0 designs were acquired by BR from many of the famous locomotive builders, including North British, Hunslet and Andrew Barclay, often in small batches for specific areas, but almost all had gone by the late-1960s. A more accurate Class 06 could be another

OTHER SCALES As well as 'OO', there is an increasingly good choice of small ready-to-run shuntir

'N' GAUGE

Steam

- Dapol GWR '57XX'/'8750' 0-6-0PT
- Dapol LBSCR/SR Stroudley 'Terrier' 0-6-0T
- Graham Farish LMS Fowler 'Jinty' 0-6-0T
- DJ Models Hunslet 'Austerity'/LNER 'J94' 0-6-0ST (in development)
- Graham Farish LNER 'J72' 0-6-0T (in development)

Diesel

- Graham Farish BR Class 03 0-6-0DM
- Graham Farish BR/Drewry Class 04 0-6-0DM
- Graham Farish BR Class 08 0-6-0DE
- N Gauge Society/Revolution Hunslet 325hp 0-6-0DH (due 2018)

popular option.

A more quirky BR shunter that has been mentioned favourably by certain suppliers of ready-to-run models is the Western Region PWM650-654 0-6-0 diesel-electric. These five small Ruston & Hornsby 'Permanent Way Machines' (PWM) were never part of the revenue earning fleet, but regarded more as on-track plant and used during civil engineering possessions and to shunt various engineers' sidings on the Western. One even ended up in Scotland in the 1990s.

On the steam front, there are many possible options for expanding the shunter fleet, but certain locomotives have a strong following, or lend themselves well to mass production.

The LMS had an interesting fleet of small 0-4-0T and 0-6-0T dock tanks, some of which were inherited from the Midland and London and North Western railways. The chunky little Fowler 0-6-0T dock tank has already been the subject of one off-the-shelf model – a Minitrix 'N' gauge product of the 1970s – but could it also work in OO?

The LNER is already fairly well-served, but one gap in the shunter fleet stands out at the moment – a Great Eastern 'J67'/'J69' 0-6-0T would undoubtedly find favour with many LNER modellers especially with the recent influx of Great Eastern motive power in the 'B12' 4-6-0, 'D16/3' 4-4-0 and 'J15' 0-6-0.

Finally, how about some new 'Pugs'?

A re-tooled LYR 0-4-0ST could be a 'winner', as could a Scottish 'Pug' of either the Caledonian Railway or North British variety.

When it comes to industrials, there's even greater scope for expansion, although demand is less certain. Another high-quality 0-6-0T steam locomotive, perhaps a Hudswell, Clarke or Manning Wardle design would fill a gap in the market. For a real challenge, how about a working 'OO' gauge model of a Ruston 48DS 4w diesel?

Whatever your preferences, there's clearly still plenty of mileage for manufacturers in this area and we look forward to seeing more 'little critters' appearing on layouts over the coming years. ■

In 2017 Heljan released a pair of GWR shunting locomotives in the '1361' 0-6-0ST (left) and '1366' 0-6-0PT (right). Both use the same chassis and feature a 6-pin DCC decoder socket.

locomotives in other scales, steam, diesel, main line and industrial.

'O' GAUGE
Steam
- Dapol GWR '57XX'/'8750' 0-6-0PT (due 2018)
- Minerva Model Railways GWR '57XX'/'8750' 0-6-0PT
- Dapol LBSCR/SR Stroudley 'Terrier' 0-6-0T
- Dapol LMS Fowler 'Jinty' 0-6-0T
- DJ Models Hunslet 'Austerity'/LNER 'J94' 0-6-0ST (in development)
- Ixion Model Railways Hudswell, Clarke 0-6-0ST
- Minerva Model Railways Kerr, Stuart 'Victory' 0-6-0T
- Minerva Model Railways Peckett 0-4-0ST

Diesel
- DJH BR Class 03 0-6-0DM
- Heljan BR Class 03 0-6-0DM (due 2018)
- Heljan Hunslet/BR Class 05 0-6-0DM
- Dapol BR Class 08 0-6-0DE
- Ixion Model Railways Fowler (GWR) 0-4-0DM
- Little Loco Co. Ruston 48DS 4wDM (due late-2017)

'Merchant' makeover

PAUL CHETTER investigates the potential for enhancing Hornby's newly tooled 'Merchant Navy' class 'Pacific' and explains several possibilities from which to select.

ALL MODELS of 'streamlined' steam locomotives have generous internal spaces and this model, first released by Hornby in March 2017, is no exception. In common with Hornby's current design philosophy, the tender is equipped with an 8-pin Digital Command Control (DCC) socket and some provision for the fitting of a 28mm round speaker. This is not surprising as Hornby's own sound offering, Twin Track Sound

(TTS) delivered in the model of 35023 *Holland-Afrika Line* (R3382TTS), uses this configuration.

The clear advantages of following this path are that there is no need to dismantle the locomotive, tenders are smaller and easier to handle, and as such work is non-destructive it will not invalidate your warranty.

Using our test bed DCC ready model of 35028 *Clan Line*, for a simple DCC installation, it could hardly be more straightforward. Release two screws, remove the tender top and DCC

blanking plug, insert the decoder plug and refit the tender top to the chassis. A standard sound installation requires, in addition to the above, the temporary displacement of the ballast weight and decoder socket, the sealing of a 28mm round speaker to the mounting position in the chassis floor and of course the use of a DCC sound decoder. Both of these are covered in the early part of the 'Step by Step' guide and show how simple it can be to introduce digital control and sound. »

Bulleid's 'Merchant Navy' 4-6-2s were stunning machines unlike anything else on the railway. In original air-smoothed form, Southern Railway built 35011 *General Steam Navigation* has a full head of steam as it steps forward from Bournemouth Central with an up express for Waterloo on May 4 1957.
T.G. Hepburn/Rail Archive Stephenson.

STEP BY STEP **INSTALLING DCC SOUND, STAY ALIVE AND LIGHTING IN A HORNBY 'MERCHANT NAVY'**

1 The Hornby-provided DCC 8-pin socket and speaker mounting are in the tender. For a simple installation, there is no need to open the locomotive at all. Access is gained by first releasing two screws at the bottom of deep recesses at the rear of the tender chassis.

The rear of the tender body can be raised to allow the two location tabs at the front to be undipped from the chassis.

3 The tabs (arrowed in red) are fairly obvious but take special note of the peg at the base of the handbrake column (arrowed in yellow). This locates in a hole in the chassis and if not correctly seated during re-assembly, the tender top will not fit properly.

4 In this shot of the tender chassis, the ballast weight, DCC socket and holes for the tabs and peg of the tender top can be seen, the latter arrowed in corresponding colours.

5 Fitting a non-sound decoder to the 8-pin socket at this point would complete a straight DCC installation, leaving only the reuniting of the tender body and chassis.

6 To add a 28mm round speaker for sound as Hornby intended, the three screws holding the ballast weight should be released, allowing the weight to be removed. This reveals the wiring arrangements, holes for the sounds to escape and partial mounting ring for the speaker.

It's important to separate the sounds emitted at the front of the speaker from those emitted from the rear otherwise performance will be severely compromised. I've used Blu Tack to fill the gaps in the mounting.

8 Fit the speaker, ensuring there's no possibility of the in-fill material fouling the speaker membrane whilst moulding to produce an airtight seal. Decoder wires were soldered to the speaker terminals whilst access was unfettered.

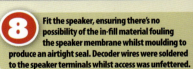

9 Reinstate the ballast weight and DCC socket. In practice, I would insulate the speaker terminals to avoid shorting, but for darity this is not shown here.

10 The MX645R decoder was plugged in, wires tidied up to reduce bulk before the tender was reassembled. This would be the last stage in a straightforward DCC sound installation.

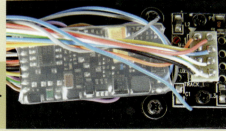

Customising

There are several other ways in which the power of a decoder can be used to customise individual models. In this case the brief was to add cab lighting and firebox flicker effects. The plan was to keep the speaker in the tender and use four Function Outputs (FOs) to provide independently operated cab lights and variable effects in the firebox. This would mean five additional wires to span the gap between locomotive and tender, a total of nine with the Hornby fitted wires. This would detract from the visual appeal but, more importantly, significantly reduce the flexibility of the joint between locomotive and tender.

Accommodating the decoder in the locomotive body, if possible, would be a practical solution to avoid introducing these potential problems.

Fortunately, there is plenty of usable space within the 'Merchant Navy' model. Cross bracing used to stiffen the body can make access to some areas less convenient but they do not compromise the actual spaces required for this conversion. Relocation of the decoder would also create enough clear space in the tender to improve the sound output by fitting a Zimo 40mm x 26mm twin driver speaker unit.

I removed the DCC socket and ballast weight to gain access to the wiring in the base of the

tender. Wires to and from the socket were disconnected and the socket discarded. There is a white 4-pin connection accessed from below the front of the tender chassis employed to carry track power to the decoder and regulated power from the decoder to the motor in the locomotive. These connections are transferred to a small Printed Circuit Board (PCB) inside the tender. The outside pair of wires is for track pick-ups. I removed the now redundant wiring from the tender pick-up PCB (fitted below the provided speaker mounting) and fixed wires between each PCB in the correct orientation.

The inner pair of wires originally carried power

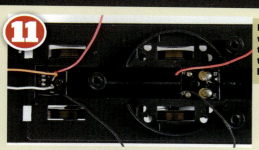

In preparation to fit only a speaker in the tender with the decoder in the locomotive, I first removed the wiring from the DCC connector then removed the shorter set of track pick-up wires from their PCB below the speaker mounting.

I used the existing wires from the outer solder pads of the forward PCB to complete the circuits with track pick-ups at the rear PCB.

The inner pair of wires, formerly to provide power to the motor in the locomotive, was fed through the ballast weight before the latter was fixed in place. The DCC socket mountings were removed from the ballast weight to give a level platform.

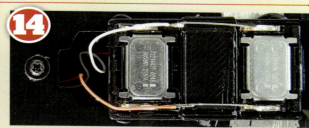

I fitted a Zimo 40mm x 26mm x 9mm twin driver speaker unit to the rear of the weight, giving clearance for the coal bunker floor, before soldering the wires to the speaker. I re-assembled the tender top and Chassis. The four-pin connector provided by Hornby to pass wiring between tender and locomotive now carries track pick-up and speaker wiring. No additional wires are required.

The locomotive body and chassis are separated by releasing three screws in total. The one shown here releases the front bogie which is hiding the second screw.

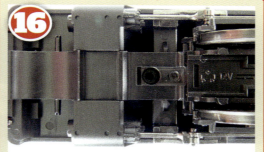

The second screw, normally residing in the recess at the centre of the picture, has been removed releasing the front of the locomotive body.

It's just possible to see the third screw, arrowed, at the bottom of this recess below the cab footplate. With all three screws removed, the body lifts away from the chassis.

The suppression capacitor seen in this overall view was removed as redundant during the installation – installing a decoder replaces its function. A number of wires run in a channel below the motor assembly, so I decided further dismantling would produce a neater result.

This close up of the flywheel, cardan shaft and gearbox illustrates the extraordinary lengths to which Hornby has gone to provide smooth vibration-free running. The flywheel has been balanced by drilling to remove material.

To begin removing the motor assembly I gently prised the top of the gearbox from its fixing tabs to reveal the worm drive.

to the motor, but as these would no longer be required with the decoder in the locomotive, I used them as speaker wires instead. With the DCC socket removed and the mounting points on the ballast weight removed with a file, the Zimo twin driver speaker fits easily in the space behind the bunker. I used mastic to fix the speaker in place then soldered the wires to it before reassembling the tender. The front steps on the tender are exposed and fragile - take care not to bend them when handing the chassis.

Following the supplied instructions, I removed three screws to release the locomotive body from the chassis. Releasing the screw holding the

front bogie reveals a hidden screw which fixes the front end of the body and chassis together. This should also be removed. At the rear, below the cab, another screw is used to retain the rear end, and must be removed. Helpfully, all three screws are of the same type and size so there is no need to make a special note of which goes where. The front retaining screw connects with a captive nut inside the body which is part of the chimney moulding. This puts paid to any idea of installing a Seuthe type smoke generator.

The first task was to rewire the chassis to provide alternative motor wires, new track pick-up to decoder connections and deploy the

replaced motor wires as speaker wires leading back via the 4-pin connector to the tender. As there was a clearly defined routing of wires below the motor mounting cradle, and to get easier access to the locomotive's track pick-up PCB, I decided to remove the motor and cradle assembly. To facilitate this, I gently prised off the top of the gearbox which also serves to retain the worm drive. This latter is driven via a motor shaft mounted flywheel and a short cardan shaft. I lifted the worm from the gearbox and disengaged the cardan shaft, putting them safely aside awaiting reassembly.

Removal of the existing wires connected to the »

STEP BY STEP | **INSTALLING DCC SOUND, STAY ALIVE AND LIGHTING IN A HORNBY 'MERCHANT NAVY'**

I lifted the worm drive from the gearbox complete with its bearings before withdrawing the cardan shaft from the flywheel.

The motor could now be removed from its mounting cradle, revealing the cradle's fixing screws and the track pick-up PCB.

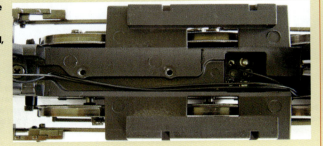

With the motor cradle removed, the wiring channel below can be seen in full. This is a very useful area in adding further functions to the 'Merchant Navy' as it keeps all the wiring secure during reassembly later.

Using a similar design to that used in the tender, the pick-up PCB incorporates a pair of spring-loaded plungers to make contact with the wheel wiper collector. The attached wires are connected to the tender pick-up wires.

I soldered a red and a black wire to the right and left hand pads respectively on the PCB. I ran these along the channel to a connector at the front of the chassis, black mastic holding them in place for a factory look.

Refitting the motor cradle ensures that these wires will never come into contact with the flywheel or cardan shaft.

The existing motor wires were removed and joined to purple speaker wires to denote their new function. Orange and grey wires were soldered to the motor terminals. These wires together with the newly added red and black pick-up wires were soldered to an 8 pin DCC socket and adhesive from a hot glue gun applied to ensure stable and electrically insulated connections.

To begin adding cab lights, I drilled a small hole above the boiler backhead in order to pass wires from a pair of DCC Concepts Nano LEDs from the cab to the inside of the model.

Threading the wires through was a modest challenge. Here the LEDs can be seen 'floating' above the firebox before fixing in place with a spot of cyano adhesive.

Although the angle of this image would suggest otherwise, the nano LEDs were fixed symmetrically above the driver and fireman's positions. These lamps can be illuminated independently and I included 10k ohms series resistors in each LED's circuit to protect from over-current and to reduce their brightness to something realistic.

motor allows it be pulled vertically from its plastic mounting cradle, revealing the two fixing screws in the base of the cradle. Releasing these allows the cradle to be removed, uncovering the special wiring channel in the chassis casting. I extended the black former motor leads with short lengths of purple speaker wire to distinguish them from the pick-up black wires when the cradle and motor were replaced.

The large space at the front allowed me to position an 8-pin socket to which I soldered the two pick-up, two motor and two speaker wires ready to accept a corresponding 8-pin plug connected to the decoder wiring which would

be fixed to the body. This arrangement would allow the body and chassis to be separated whenever required without disturbing the harnesses. I applied a little adhesive from a hot glue gun to add stability and provide insulation to the connected wires.

Body modifications

Moving to the locomotive body, I drilled a small hole from inside the body through to the cab. This allowed me to thread the single strand wires from a pair of DCC Concepts Protowhite Nano LEDs. I fixed each LED to the cab roof, roughly above the driver and fireman's positions,

with a drop of cyano adhesive.

Inside the body, I soldered a 10K ohms resistor to the negative (shorter) wire from each LED and fixed them and the wires to the body with cyano adhesive to protect the delicate single strands. The other ends of the resistors were soldered to separate function output wires from the decoder. The positive wire from each LED was connected to a common positive (blue) wire.

I created a small box from scraps of styrene sheet to serve as a dummy firebox, which I fitted with an amber LED cut from a strip of three. This already had a protective series resistor in circuit. I used the adhesive backing to fix it in place.

Intermediate
Beginner SKILL LEVEL Advanced

31 To house the firebox flicker effect, I made up a small box from scrap styrene sheet. I fitted an amber LED cut from a strip to provide the bright glow of a fire in a hard working locomotive.

32 A pair of red LEDs, connected in parallel to each other but separately from the amber LED, would provide the redder glow from a more subdued fire.

33 From inside the cab I drilled, then enlarged, a hole in the centre of the firebox doors.

34 From inside the body I cut a rectangular opening to accommodate the illuminated dummy firebox.

35 Shown here during a dry run, the firebox, complete with LEDs and wiring, was test fitted.

36 This view will rarely be seen when the tender is attached. The red LEDs are each side of the firehole out of sight. The amber LED can be seen but at normal viewing angles it will not be in direct line of sight.

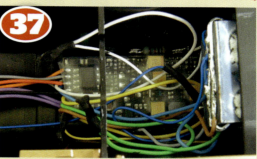

37 The decoder was fixed to the inner roof above the firebox after all connections to the firebox and cab lights had been completed. Motor, pick-up and speaker wires were passed forward to an 8-pin plug at the front of the body, ready for connection to the socket on the chassis during re-assembly.

38 A reliable power supply is essential for DCC operating. One way to ensure this is to carry some on board. 'Stay alive' capacitors charge up on the always live DCC track, but their stored power can be used to augment or temporarily replace this when supply is disrupted. The Zimo MX645 decoder has onboard capacitor management circuitry, so I made up a pack of six 2.7v 1 Farad supercapacitors wired in series to give 166,666μF at 16.2v.

39 The decoder's new 8-pin plug and the insulated 'stay alive' pack fit easily in the smokebox. The blue (+ve) and grey (-ve) wires connected to the 'stay alive' pack are provided on the decoder as standard.

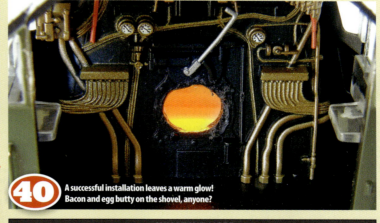

40 A successful installation leaves a warm glow! Bacon and egg butty on the shovel, anyone?

WHAT WE USED		
PRODUCT	**SUPPLIER**	**PRICE**
Zimo MX645R sound decoder	www.digitrains.co.uk	£95
Zimo LS 40mm x 26mm x 09mm (twin) speaker	www.digitrains.co.uk	£18.00
Six x 2.7v 1 F Supercapacitor Pack	www.digitrains.co.uk	£10.00
Protowhite Nano LEDs (6 Pack)	www.dccconcepts.com	£13.00

A pair of red 12v LEDs were fitted through the lower sides of the firebox.

I planned to use the different colours and brightness of the three LEDs to represent the fire in various states of combustion, to be automatically adjusted by using the decoder to match the exhaust sounds. This would be set up in the sound project before I loaded it to the decoder.

Working from the cab, I drilled a hole in the centre of the firebox doors, which I enlarged to an oval shape representing the firebox throat. From inside the body, I cut a rectangular hole to accept the dummy firebox with a snug, interference fit. After connecting the respective wires to the decoder and testing the fitted LEDs, I installed the dummy firebox.

Staying alive

As the Zimo MX645 is equipped with circuitry and wiring to connect and manage a 'stay alive' capacitor, the model was destined to operate on an exhibition layout and as there was ample free space to accommodate it, I soldered together six x 2.7v 1 Farad supercapacitors in series to provide a boost to the locomotive when needed. This pack was connected to the decoder's dedicated 'external storage wires', protected with electricians' insulation tape and fixed with sticky mastic to the inner side wall in the smokebox area of the body.

The pick-up, motor and speaker wires from the decoder were fed to the front of the body and an 8-pin plug connected to mirror the wiring of the socket located on the chassis harness, hot glue again being used to add strength and insulation.

With the plug and socket firmly locked together, I replace the body and secured it in place with the three screws removed earlier. Joining the 4-pin plug to the connector in the base of the tender and fitting the drawbar completed the installation. ■

Multi-scale
WAGON BUILD

Looking to build your first wagon kit, but don't know which scale to choose? **MIKE WILD** assembles Parkside Models' BR 24.5ton mineral wagon in 'N', 'OO' and 'O' gauge to assess the difference between scales.

Above: Three identical wagons in three different scales. I was impressed at how all three went together, but there is a great deal of satisfaction in completing an 'O' gauge wagon with its sprung couplings and buffers. Whichever you were to choose, with care they assemble into good looking, detailed and smooth-running wagons which will bring a distinctive vehicle to your train formations.

THE RECENT INFLUX of 'O' gauge ready-to-run and my decision to try my hand at modelling in 7mm:1ft scale has brought me back to a pastime I used to love – wagon kit construction.

Over the years, I've built a lot of wagons, but what struck me most about my most recent endeavours in 'O' gauge is that all six of the wagons I've built so far have run perfectly first time and without any adjustment. By contrast, I gave up on building 'N' gauge wagon kits many years ago – the last time I built an item of rolling stock in the smaller scale I was probably still a teenager. In 'OO' gauge I've had mixed success, mostly down to the weight of kit built wagons needing to be increased for good running on the track.

All this got me thinking about what I could do now. I've improved my skills and, perhaps, slowed myself down a little to make the most of a model rather than rushing it – and that's something I've only really gained from moving into 'O' gauge and modelling purely for myself (most of the time at least).

So, having decided I needed to test my skills across three scales, I also felt I could bring something useful to the table to explain their positives and negatives.

As ever, with plastic kit construction the body is the easy part – in most cases not even as difficult as a classic Airfix Spitfire with most four-wheel wagons requiring assembly of a box at their heart – but what sets a wagon apart from a static model is the need for it to run

successfully on the track. That is something that can be tricky and it is worth taking your time to check that the axles are both running parallel and true before committing to the detail components of chassis construction.

Armed with cutting mat, craft knife, sanding boards, tweezers, pliers, and a willingness to take my time over the chassis, I set about building the three wagons you see here – all modelling the 1953 introduced BR 24.5ton mineral wagon of which 2,150 were built. They operated across the BR network, but are best known for service in South Wales where block rakes were hauled in the Valleys carrying coal traffic for onward distribution. Ultimately they were replaced by HAA merry-go-round

hoppers, but the last weren't withdrawn until the early 1980s.

Each kit, all drawn from the Parkside Dundas range which has recently been purchased by Peco and rebranded as Parkside Models, was rewarding for a different reason and the 'N' gauge one especially as it is hands down the best running 'N' gauge wagon kit I think I've ever built… ■

WHAT WE USED			
PRODUCT	SCALE	CAT NO.	PRICE
BR 24.5ton mineral wagon	'N'	PN02	£8.95
BR 24.5ton mineral wagon	'OO'	PC04	£8.25
BR 24.5ton mineral wagon	'O'	PS25	£36.50

USEFUL LINKS	
Lifecolor Paints	www.airbrushes.com
Parkside Models	www.peco-uk.com
Deluxe Materials	www.gaugemaster.com
Modelmaster Decals	www.modelmaster.uk

Below: **Introduced in 1953, 2,150 BR 24.5ton mineral wagons were built with many lasting into the 1970s and the last being withdrawn in 1982. On April 7 1964, newly built Class 37 D6935 approaches Dinas Powis with 6T58 – an up train of empties formed almost entirely of 24.5ton mineral wagons.** Sid Rikard/Railphotoprints.co.uk.

TOOLS AND GLUES

» Craft knife
» Cutting mat
» Sanding boards
» Deluxe Materials Plastic Magic liquid plastic cement
» Snipe nose pliers
» Lifecolor BR freight grey (UA818)

1

The starting point for the project is these three kits from Parkside Dundas to build models of the BR 24.5ton mineral wagon. The difference: they cover 'N', 'OO' and 'O' scales.

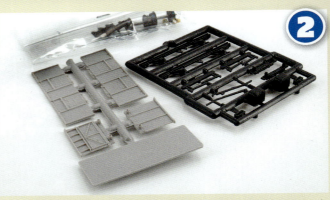

2

First to be opened is the 'N' gauge kit and what strikes me about this is just how small the parts are and, secondly, how few there are. The finished model is just 55mm long and weighs only a few grams.

3

Next up is the 'OO' gauge kit which, remarkably, is very similar in the number of components and their arrangement as the 'N' gauge kit. This time though there are more separate items to assemble to the chassis while the body construction is largely identical, except for the separate bufferbeams.

4

Finally, here are the contents of the 'O' gauge 24.5ton mineral wagon and there are noticeably more of them. Also significant is that the 'O' gauge kits from Parkside Dundas come with transfers included in the box, making completion one step simpler. There are a lot more components to the chassis though and the option to introduce compensation to the axles if required.

5

6

Deluxe Materials Plastic Magic has been my glue of choice for plastic kits since I was first introduced to it more than a decade ago. The formula has been changed, but it still provides the same strong and resilient joints it always has.

Starting with the 'O' gauge wagon body, the large sprue connections are easier to deal with using a pair of side cutters, although a craft knife with a sharp blade will do the same job. Either way, take care not to damage the wagon side and be prepared to clean the tabs up with a sanding board afterwards.

7

Building up the bodyshell is much the same through all three scales, but you need small fingers for the 'N' gauge model. Here I've assembled three sides to the floor allowing them to cure for an hour before adding the fourth. The result should be a strong and rigid box.

8

Cutting the parts from the sprues for the 'N' and 'OO' models should be done with a craft knife. Don't feel you should cut right by the wagon side – in fact it is often better to cut part-way down the tab and clean it up after removal when you have better access from all angles.

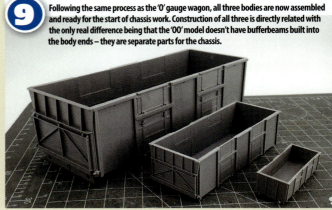

9

Following the same process as the 'O' gauge wagon, all three bodies are now assembled and ready for the start of chassis work. Construction of all three is directly related with the only real difference being that the 'OO' model doesn't have bufferbeams built into the body ends – they are separate parts for the chassis.

Intermediate
Beginner **SKILL LEVEL** Advanced

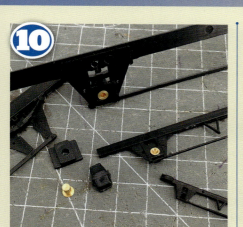

10

The chassis is where most of the differences become obvious and particularly in the axleboxes. The 'N' gauge model has no brass bearing (lower right) while the 'OO' model has axleboxes moulded as part of the underframe sides and a separate bearing to insert (centre right). The 'O' gauge model has three-piece axleboxes – outer, inner, and bearing – which fit into slots in the 'W' irons on the underframe side. These are designed so that they can slide up and down in the hornblocks, giving the wagon a degree of suspension should you wish.

11 Focusing on the 'N' gauge wagon, we can bring it to completion in three steps now. First, the chassis sides are checked and assembled to the wagon floor with the wheelsets in place. The ends of each side needed a tiny trim to fit comfortably between the bufferbeams. Check that the wheels can rotate freely while the glue will still allow adjustment.

12

Next the brake gear, consisting of four components, is installed. This involves fitting the brake shoe moulding between the wheels on each side and the brake levers too. Make sure you add the right lever to the right side of the wagon as they are handed.

13

The final step in 'N' gauge body construction – apart from couplings which we will come to later – is addition of the brass buffers. Add a tiny spot of Plastic Magic glue into the holes and press the buffers into place. Simple. This wagon is now ready for painting.

14

Going up a scale to 'OO' gauge, the main chassis is formed of four parts – two bufferbeams and two sides. One side requires removal of the second smaller triangle hanger to suit the handed brake lever arrangement. It is essential at this stage to check the wagon rolls freely.

15 The brake gear components can be cut from the sprue next and cleaned up ready for installation. These are the four main pieces which fit as per the 'N' gauge model.

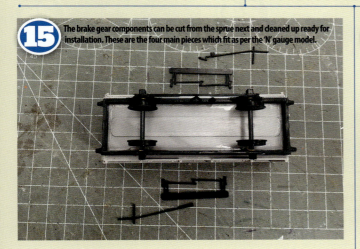

16 To finish the 'OO' wagon body, we added the plastic buffer heads and dummy screw coupling hooks. Standing it side by side with the 'N' gauge version, there is very little to choose between them in terms of construction other than their size.

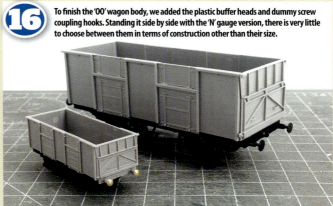

17

Now we are moving onto the 'O' gauge chassis which offers the opportunity to install much more detail to the underframe. These are the brake system components, all of which needed to be fitted to the previously attached underframe sides and central structure.

18 The triangular hangers are fitted first to attach the brake levers to.

STEP BY STEP **ASSEMBLING BR 24.5 TON MINERAL WAGONS IN 'N', 'OO' AND 'O'**

Next, after trimming of the brake shoes for a clear fit, the brake shoe supports and moulding are installed, ensuring they don't foul on the wheels.

Finally, the brake levers are added on both sides together with the ratchet supports at their outer ends to complete the chassis.

The buffers for the 'O' gauge kit are fully sprung and start off as five separate components: a turned metal buffer, plastic collar, spring, buffer shank and a brass nut. These are assembled by sliding the collar onto the buffer followed by the spring. This assembly is then fed into the shank and the nut wound onto the thread from the rear. The collar can then be carefully glued in place to finish.

22 The buffers press through pre-drilled holes in the bufferbeam and are secured in place with a small amount of Plastic Magic. These are surprisingly therapeutic to assemble and fit.

We now have three completed wagons awaiting two more processes: addition of couplings and painting. The sheer size difference between the 'N' and 'O' gauge models is clear to see here.

Couplings for the 'N' gauge wagon are based on a Peco design. They are simple to assemble, but care needs to be taken not to allow glue into the coupling mount body. They fix to the underside of the body between two locating lugs once assembled.

In 'OO', we opted not to use the supplied couplings instead adding NEM couplings using adapters made by Chivers Finelines – although these appear to be temporarily unavailable. Using them involves a pair of cranked Bachmann couplings to get the correct coupling height.

The idea of making three-link couplings initially put me off 'O' gauge wagon kits, but they aren't as difficult as you might think. At the top is a completed coupling and below are the component parts.

To assemble the links, I open one with a pair of snipe nose pliers and put the other two links on it before closing it up again. That gives me the trio of links.

I then open up one of the outer links and thread the coupling hook itself onto the trio before closing it up using the same tools.

Intermediate

Beginner **SKILL LEVEL** Advanced

Resembling a Russian doll in model form, the three wagons show their respective sizes off stacked inside one another.

 The brass coupling hook can now be posted through the gap in the bufferbeam – this one didn't even need cleaning out – before the wagon is turned over to complete its installation.

 Thread the spring on the coupling bar then spread the split at the back of the coupling bar to keep it in place using small snipe nose pliers. I find fitting couplings like this quite satisfying, and it brings each build to a conclusion.

Masterpieces in the
GALLERY

Selected from hundreds of images which made up *Hornby Magazine's* layout features in 2017, we present a selection of the best layouts and model photography from the past year.

Rays of light burst through the roof of the half roundhouse at 45C Westlands on a bright spring afternoon. Riddles 'WD' 2-8-0s fill the shed as a lone 'spotter' collects the numbers while hoping to find a gleaming 'Pacific' for his ABC too. This stunning 'OO' shed layout has been built by a group of retired Royal Marines with the purpose of supporting ex-servicemen as well as promoting the hobby. It launched in November 2016 on display at Tesco in Crewe and has since become a popular part of the exhibition circuit. 45C Westlands featured in HM125.
Trevor Jones/*Hornby Magazine*.

Bill Wood set out to model the famous West Highland Line in 'OO' gauge focusing on the Mallaig extension in the 1980s. It might not include the famous concrete viaduct at Glenfinnan, but this model has all the charm and character of the real location and the right motive power too. A BR blue Class 26/0 ambles towards the station with a short rake of 12ton box vans representing a typical short goods from the era. Glenfinnan featured in HM118.
Nigel Burkin/Hornby Magazine.

The turntable at Old Oak Common depot in London prompted Steve Pike to create Seven Ash in 'OO' – a superb portrayal of a busy Western Region open air depot in the 1970s transition era when hydraulics were beginning to give way to diesel-electric power on the region. Faded blue, maroon with full yellow ends, BR green and a variety of warning panel styles were all part of daily life. Seven Ash featured in HM125. *Trevor Jones/Hornby Magazine.*

Gowerton Parkway models the Great Western Main Line in South Wales in the early 2000s in 'OO'. Marcus Lambert took over the loft of his home to create this permanent layout which includes a continuous run with four-sided scenery as well as a storage yard accessed by a triangular junction. A First Great Western HST draws in on the main line as a Class 153 waits for passengers to transfer to continue their journey. Gowerton Parkway featured in HM123. *Trevor Jones/Hornby Magazine.*

Eric Austin used his visits to the scenic Paignton and Dartmouth Steam Railway as the inspiration for his busy Great Western Railway theme terminus in 'OO' gauge. Set firmly in the BR steam era it features operation aplenty including the station, goods sidings and shed area too. Here a '57XX' 0-6-0PT is engaged in shunting while a 'Grange' 4-6-0 moves towards the turntable and a '45XX' 2-6-2T arrives with a terminating passenger service. Dart Valley Junction featured in **HM116.** *Trevor Jones/Hornby Magazine.*

Leicester (Belgrave Road) is Abingdon and District MRC's busy Great Northern theme terminus which includes intensive passenger and freight movements to keep the operators on their toes. This impressive exhibition layout is a regular on the circuit and took part in the *Hornby Magazine* sponsored Great Electric Train Show in October 2017. Leicester (Belgrave Road) featured in **HM121.** *Trevor Jones/Hornby Magazine.*

The Western Region's Aller Junction near Newton Abbot caught the eye of Chris Morris after he purchased a Dapol 'N' gauge 'Western' as D1000 *Western Enterprise* in desert sand livery. From that moment he was hooked and went on to develop this busy little layout which fits a junction, inclines, main line movements and a storage yard into 7ft x 3ft. Here a North British Class 22 has just been given the road after a 'Hymek' has crossed with a van train. Little Aller Junction featured in HM123. *Mike Wild/Hornby Magazine.*

Bilston Road is what many modellers dream of – a big main line layout with four-sided scenery, two storage yards and space to run scale length trains, and all in 'OO' gauge too. Geoff Read has built the layout over the past 10 years since moving to a new house where he was able to add a purpose built railway room in the loft. Here a BR '9F' 2-10-0 heads a long rake of 14ton Esso oil tankers, complete with the obligatory barrier wagons at the front, through the country scene. Bilston Road featured in HM119. *Mike Wild/Hornby Magazine.*

Overhauling TWELVE TREES

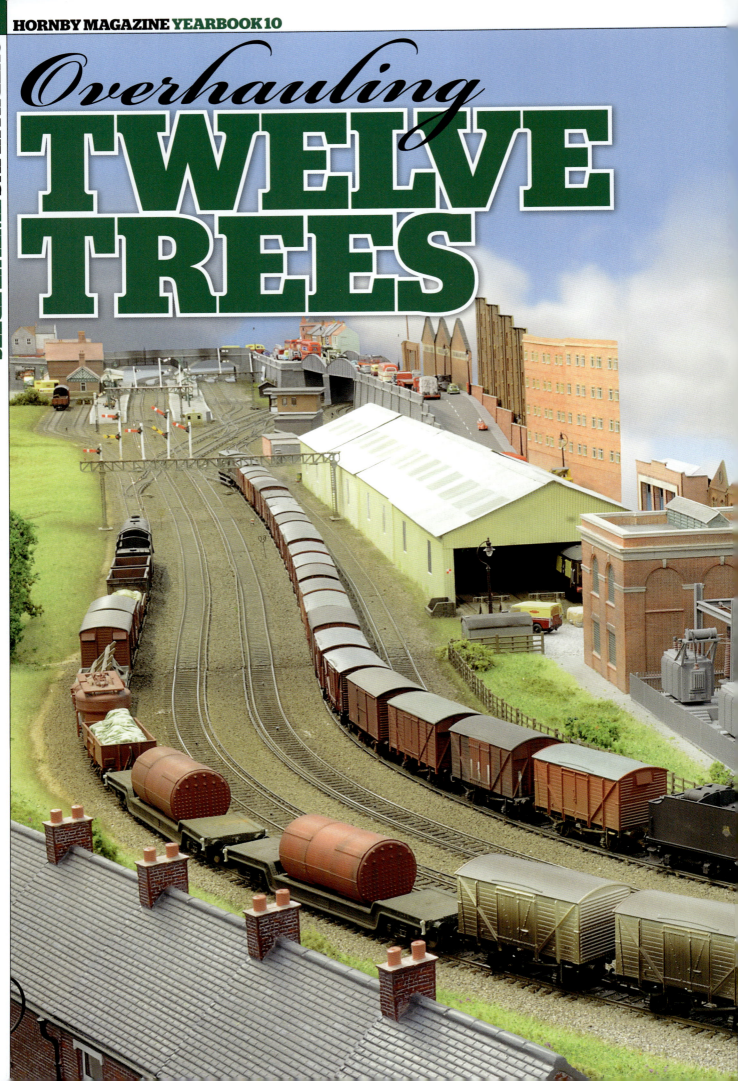

Over a three-month period, the *Hornby Magazine* team set about rebuilding and reviving its largest exhibition layout for a return to the show circuit at the Great Electric Train Show. **MIKE WILD** reveals what has been done and how the team have delivered and enhanced the finished product.

PHOTOGRAPHY, MIKE WILD AND TREVOR JONES

Visitors gather at Twelve Trees while the operating team ensure that the trains have clear routes through the scenic area.

WHEN WE BUILD a new model railway, we sometimes throw caution to the wind and develop a scheme for its impact on the scenic side while leaving the operational part of the equation for later. Twelve Trees Junction falls firmly into that camp.

This substantial Southern Region layout was built for *Hornby Magazine Yearbook No. 6* in 2013, but it was another 12 months before it made its debut at an exhibition. It is by far the largest and most complex layout we have built so far and part of its impact was also its biggest weakness – the storage yards. To save time in making the layout available for its first exhibition season, we developed a set of cassette yards to support

A Hornby Maunsell 'S15' 4-6-0, fitted with a Zimo MX645 sound decoder and LS40x22 twin driver speaker, heads a long fitted van train through Twelve Trees Junction and past the new Faller transformer station on the new scenic board.

the three main connections to the scenic area, but this meant that the scenic area was almost dwarfed by the length of the off-scene yards – each end having a 9ft long area - and we had a labour-intensive system to provide the trains. It worked, but it was hard going during a full weekend on show and, quite honestly, the scenic side was being under-supplied with trains because we couldn't turn them around quickly enough to allow a constant and consistent flow.

Another plan which was proposed was a pair of return loop storage yards, one at each end, but again this extended the length of the layout significantly with non-scenic boards. We wanted the scenery to dominate rather than the storage yard, so it was back to the drawing board.

After attending three shows with the cassette yards, all of which were successful, for various reasons Twelve Trees was stood down and placed into storage while other layouts from our portfolio took the limelight including Shortley Bridge and Felton Cement Works (*Yearbook No. 7*), West Riding Power (*Yearbook No. 8*) and Grosvenor Square (*Yearbook No. 9*). However, the big Southern layout still held great interest for the team and its reception at shows gave us new impetus to bring it back to life and prepare it to become our flagship layout once more.

Revival plan

The original 16ft x 3ft scenic section remains at the heart of the revised layout which consists of a main line station, approaching goods loops, double track main line junction and associated web of pointwork along with a collection of Electric Multiple Unit (EMU) carriage sidings. All the Peco code 75 track is fitted with third-rail electrification, apart from the bay platform, using Peco Individulay code 60 rail and insulator pots.

The period is focused on the years 1955-1967 with a few exceptions, although lately it has been moving more towards the 1960-1967 era allowing the final years of Maunsell locomotive operation to run side by side with the new introductions of early diesel locomotives and the first BR blue liveried multiple units. Trains on the original version were restricted to seven carriages or 20 wagons (plus a locomotive in each case) to fit within the length of the cassette yards and this also presented operational problems as specific cassettes were required to receive and despatch the eight-car 4-CEP formation which operates on the layout. This » we wanted to change so that we had absolute flexibility over train lengths and so that the full scale block freights could be operated.

The revival plan started with what could be considered a modest requirement: to take the layout into a continuous run format with a storage yard at the rear to provide a more consistent flow of trains. It was also aimed at increasing the range of trains available on the track while also reducing stock handling during a show. Having drawn the scheme out, the overall size of the layout changed dramatically from its original 34ft x 8ft total footprint to one which covers 24ft x 10ft. In turn, this change in format also gave rise for expansion of the scenic area at each end meaning that the original 16ft length would benefit from two further 4ft x 3ft baseboards either end of the existing scenery to give a total 24ft long scene. That's no bad thing when we were also aiming to increase train lengths in many cases up to eight vehicles and also to allow some of the longer block trains to operate such as a 24-wagon cement train, a block oil service of Heljan Class B 35ton tankers and others.

Recovery team

The next phase of the plan was to work out what we could reuse or recover from the original layout. We needed to keep one of the cassette yards to work with Grosvenor Square, where it provides much needed additional capacity, but on the upside, the other two original cassette yards could provide a great deal of materials for the rebuild.

Firstly, four of the 4ft x 2ft baseboards would be repurposed as the straight 16ft long storage yard boards for the rear of the revised layout while all but six of the cassettes could have their code 75 track reclaimed to be relaid in the new yard. This gave us a flying start on the project and with the stripping of the storage yard for our disbanded Western Region branch line layout, St Stephens Road, we were also able to acquire 25 points for reuse on the new yard. This gave a considerable cost saving and while a couple of the points proved to be at the end of their working lives, all the rest have been either used or set aside for future layout projects.

To build the remainder of the new yard meant starting from scratch with a total of six 4ft x 3ft baseboards being required to create new ends to join the straight scenic and yard boards together.

Perhaps one of the most challenging aspects was working out how the double junction could

Mike Wild (left) and Graham Muspratt (right) take control of the inner main lines through the new continuous run storage yard for Twelve Trees. At the centre is the twin screen computer set up operating Hornby's RailMaster software for point control.

be rejoined with the main lines at the rear without having separate storage yards. Fortunately, the length of the new yard meant it was possible to do this without losing out on train storage with the final design being capable of holding two seven-coach trains and locomotives on each of the 10 storage tracks or a combination of longer and shorter sets depending on requirements.

Summer project

Physical construction started in mid-July with the arrival of the storage yard boards in the *Hornby Magazine* workshop for repurposing. Having removed the original connection panels from

the top of the baseboards, all the surfaces were painted with matt grey emulsion paint for a consistent finish – grey now being our standard colour for presentation – and DCC Concepts alignment dowels were fitted between each pair of boards for consistent set up of the layout at shows. These make a huge difference to erecting the layout and are a product that we won't be building any future layouts without.

Next, tracklaying started in earnest, beginning with the complex junction at the yard throat to create the links with the two main line route options. Plain track followed for the rest of these boards and very quickly we had four new boards

The starting point: the original cassette yard boards are assembled ready for stripping, painting and fitting of alignment dowels.

Track is mocked up to ensure that the 11 tracks required for the design can be accommodated on the 2ft wide boards.

Point work is planned out on the new boards to ensure that all the required components are available and will fit correctly.

DCC Concepts alignment dowels have been fitted to all of the new and reclaimed baseboards for the storage yard.

fully completed with track. Time restrictions meant it was the end of August before it was all wired, tested and ready for the next phase of development, putting us on the back foot on our schedule to meet the Great Electric Train Show deadline.

Come September and we had just six weeks to go until the layout's debut in its new format so two days were set aside to accelerate construction of the missing baseboards and to assemble the layout in full prior to track work being progressed. On the first of those days, all six of the new boards were built, painted and, after being left for the glue and paint to dry for

12 hours, we were back in the workshop the next day for an intensive session to put everything together including fitting of DCC Concepts alignment dowels to all the new boards and initial track connections between the original scenic area and the new sections. Happily, by the end of the day the entire layout was in one piece, and assembled outside the workshop, just in time for it to be dismantled again.

We then began an intensive programme of track laying on one half of the layout, focusing on the junction end first which used more than 50 yards of track along with hundreds of rail joiners and track pins. The link board between the

junction and the new yard was built too and set in place and by September 17, 12 days after the new boards had been built, we had trains running around the junction end of the layout into the first half of the storage yard. Completing this area was installation of 24 DCC Concepts Cobalt IP digital point motors, which were selected for their speed of installation, reliability and simple programming options.

New scenics

The junction end was packed down within 24 hours of completion and the London end of the layout and its new baseboards were put »

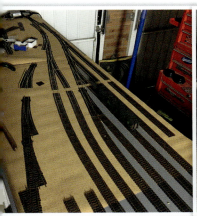

With the baseboards painted 1/16th in thick cork is laid under the track for consistency with the scenic boards.

All in a day's work - four of the six new 4ft x 3ft storage yard boards have been assembled here with the final two in preparation.

Testing the complete layout's assembly required a dry day! It doesn't quite fit in the workshop.

OVERHAULING TWELVE TREES

together in the workshop instead, taking us into the final phase of the redevelopment with just under three weeks to go until the Great Electric Train Show – and we had decided to take the plunge and extend the scenery by 4ft in the process at this end too.

Track work was handled quickly and within six days of the boards being put together, only working in the evenings and at weekends, all the track was laid, wired and tested. The remaining 12 DCC Concepts Cobalt motors were installed shortly after leaving the way clear for us to develop the scenery and other finishing elements in time for the show.

The starting point for the scenery was relocation of the original road bridge which formed the scenic break after the carriage sheds. This was quickly released from its original position and established, at least, where the trains would exit and arrive from. Next, we decided on a row of houses at the front of the layout set on a raised embankment above the railway using Hornby terrace houses. Behind we wanted something different and after finding a low-relief frontage for a stone factory in our stores to continue the backscene theme, we went in search of a transformer station to create a sub-station for the third-rail power supply.

Having researched the options, we found the ideal kit in a product from the Faller 'HO' scale range available through Gaugemaster. Allied with a Bachmann Scenecraft substation building, we had all the components we needed and started the scenic process by weathering the track with Humbrol No. 29 from an aerosol before ballasting with a combination of Woodland Scenics fine and medium grade blended grey ballasts. This was fixed in place with diluted PVA before being left to cure for 24 hours.

The raised bed for the houses and road came next using 9mm plywood supported on 18mm deep strips of planed timber. This gave a small rise above the railway, but not too much. Charcoal coloured artists' mounting card was used for the road surface and we then went on to build up the embankment between the railway and road areas using scrunched up newspaper overlaid with a web of masking tape. This was then covered with squares of newspaper painted with a coat of PVA glue building up half a dozen layers to give a strong, but quick to create and cheap to source, landscape. Once dry this was painted brown as a base colour for grasses.

WHAT WE USED		
PRODUCT	MANUFACTURER	CAT NO.
Code 75 medium left	Peco	SL-E196
Code 75 medium right	Peco	SL-E195
Code 75 large left	Peco	SL-E189
Code 75 large right	Peco	SL-E188
Code 75 curved left	Peco	SL-E187
Code 75 curved right	Peco	SL-E186
Code 75 live frog diamond crossing	Peco	SL-E194
Code 75 large 'Y'	Peco	SL-E198
Code 75 rail joiners	Peco	SL-110
Code 75 insulated rail joiners	Peco	SL-111
Code 75 wooden sleepered track	Peco	SL-100F
Track pins	Peco	ST-280
Alignment dowels	DCC Concepts	DCB-DOWEL
Cork sheet, 36in x 24in	Gaugemaster	GM130
9mm plywood	Various	n/a
69mm x 18mm planed timber	Various	n/a
4.0 x 35mm twin thread wood screws	Reiser	n/a
4.0 x 20mm twin thread wood screws	Reiser	n/a
Terrace house, left	Hornby	R8621
Terrace house, right	Hornby	R8622
Sub-station	Bachmann	44-069
Southern Region concrete platelayer's hut	Hornby	R9512
Low relief church	Hornby	R9757
Code 60 rail	Peco	IL-6
Insulator pots	Peco	IL-120
Cobalt IP digital point motor	DCC Concepts	DCP-CB1DiP
Copper clad sleeper strip, 4mm x 1mm	C&L Finescale	4ZC101B
Transformer station	Faller	130958
Medium grade blended grey ballast	Woodland Scenics	B1393
Fine grade blended grey ballast	Woodland Scenics	B1394
York paving strips	Wills	SS77
Black swan neck lamps	Gaugemaster	GM816
Blended green fine turf	Woodland Scenics	T1349
Spring/summer/autumn static grass, long	Green Scene	Various
Spring/summer/autumn static grass, medium	Green Scene	Various
Light green coarse turf	Woodland Scenics	T1363
Burnt grass coarse turf	Woodland Scenics	T1362
Light green fine leaf foliage	Woodland Scenics	F1132
Olive green fine leaf foliage	Woodland Scenics	F1133
Spear fencing	Ratio	434
Spear fencing ramps and gates	Ratio	435
Lineside fencing	Ratio	425
Block paving	Redutex	076AC211

Paving around the street scene is Wills York paving sections painted with grey primer (and now in need of toning down with weathering) while the church has been set in with a path cut from Wills York paving sheet surrounded by Woodland Scenics blended grey ballasts. Ratio spear fencing finishes this area including a partially open gate, although there is plenty of scope for future detailing here with cameo scenes.

The sub-station was assembled as per the instructions in the Faller kit, but following research of British prototypes, it became clear that the entire structure needed painting in grey rather than the supplied green. This was sprayed onto the whole transformer station, using standard grey primer which was then detailed with Lifecolor Fitted Freight bauxite »

The junction end of the layout has an intensive track formation which swallowed over 50 yards of track.

Point formations give multiple route options for the additional storage loops on the inner circuits.

At the London end progress began with movement of the original road bridge to its new location and mocking up of the main buildings.

As Kernow's Bulleid diesel thunders through with the 'Bournemouth Belle' a Bulleid 'Q1' 0-6-0 heads a ballast train towards the capital. All trains are driven on Gaugemaster Prodigy handsets.

Track into the other end of the storage yard is simpler, but still complex and intensive.

A pair of additional crossovers were added to the plan at the yard entrance to increase flexibility in train movements.

With the new backscene temporarily in place the area for scenic treatment is clear. The track has been weathered with Humbrol No. 29.

The new main line is ballasted with matching Woodland Scenics blended grey colours to go with the original layout. It will need weathering.

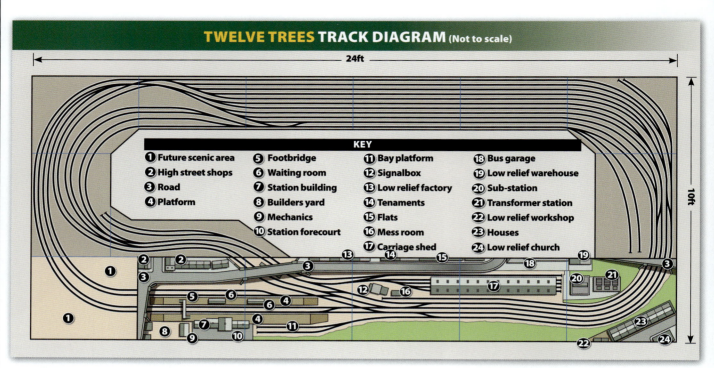

TWELVE TREES TRACK DIAGRAM (Not to scale)

24ft

10ft

KEY

❶ Future scenic area	❺ Footbridge	⓫ Bay platform	⓲ Bus garage
❷ High street shops	❻ Waiting room	⓬ Signalbox	⓳ Low relief warehouse
❸ Road	❼ Station building	⓭ Low relief factory	⓴ Sub-station
❹ Platform	❽ Builders yard	⓮ Tenaments	㉑ Transformer station
	❾ Mechanics	⓯ Flats	㉒ Low relief workshop
	❿ Station forecourt	⓰ Mess room	㉓ Houses
		⓱ Carriage shed	㉔ Low relief church

for the insulators together with Worn Black while final weathering was added using ComArt Light Dust filter colours to soften the primer grey aerosol finish. It will benefit from further weathering in the future, but we didn't want to go too far during our initial short build time.

To finish the scenic area, ground cover followed our time-honoured method of Woodland Scenics blended green fine turf for the base colour with two layers of static grass from Green Scene applied on top once it had dried to increase the depth of ground cover. This was further embellished with detailed grass turfs and colours to create the final look with these final layers being fixed in place with extra hold hairspray.

As part of the rebuild, we also introduced a new low-relief entrance to the bus garage along the backscene as well as completing painting of the brick walling around the depot sidings. Redutex paving was introduced around the base of the brick substation building as well as the stone factory frontage as finishing touches.

The final piece of the scenic jigsaw was the addition of third rail on the new main lines which involved fitting 170 insulator pots to 10ft of code 60 rail and drilling 1mm diameter holes to suit. However, we also realised a mistake as we

had fixed the road bridge down before drilling the holes for the insulator pots. To work around this, we cut down a pin vice so it would fit underneath the bridge to make the final dozen holes required to complete the third rail.

Weathering of the track and ballast with Geoscenics Track Grime and Black Concentrate, let down with water in each case, followed making the new baseboard ready to pack into the van with the others by 4pm on the Thursday before the show – just in time.

On show

Now we had a completed layout packed and loaded into the van. The stock had been checked and tested and we had a large number of new additions to the roster including four Class 71s, three Class 73s, a 4-TC, a pair of air-smoothed 'Merchant Navy' 4-6-2s, a Drummond '700' 0-6-0, a Maunsell 'S15' 4-6-0, Adams 'O2' 0-4-4T and more besides. The carriage fleet had been expanded to included Hornby's Maunsell 58ft non-corridor stock, a Bachmann 'Birdcage' set and a rake of Hornby 12-wheel Pullman cars which had been waiting for their moment. We also had special guests for the layout for its first weekend back on show including production samples of the Kernow Bulleid diesel 10201 as

well as LSWR 'Gate stock' from the same source together with a Wainwright 'H' 0-4-4T from Hornby and, arriving on the Saturday morning, decorated but un-motorised samples of the Hatton's Wainwright 'P' 0-6-0T.

However, we also had a layout which hadn't been tested, a new control system which needed shaking down and a lot of final preparations to make on the Friday night. Assembly of the main layout was quick and painless and we soon had everything built up and the extended 20ft long lighting rig assembled with its new gallows for extra support. The first trains ran around late on the Friday evening, leaving the finishing jobs for the morning ready for the doors opening to the public at 9.30am. This included setting up 25 trains in the storage yard together with a group of multiple units in the carriage sidings meaning that we had over 30 formations on track and ready to run.

Control of the layout had been moved on from the original Gaugemaster Prodigy system which we operated the trains and points from initially. We retained the Gaugemaster system for train operation – with the addition of DCC Specialities circuit breakers for each half of the storage yard – but point control was handed over to an entirely separate system using a Hornby Elite connected

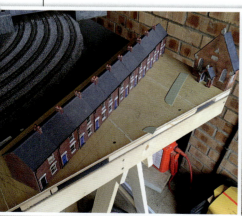

Hornby terrace houses are raised above the railway on a separate plinth made from 9mm plywood supported by 18mm deep planed timber.

The embankment between the railway and the houses is made from newspaper overlaid with masking tape and finished with PVA coated squares of newspaper.

The landscape is taking shape, but there is still much to do with just five days to go until the show when this image was taken.

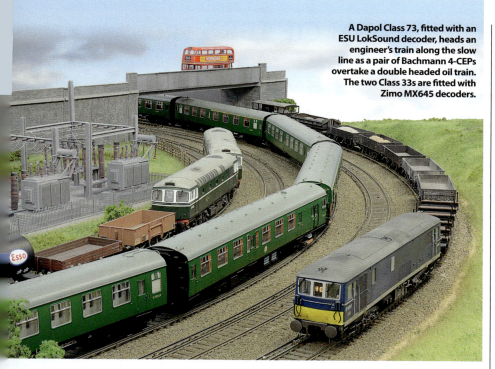

A Dapol Class 73, fitted with an ESU LokSound decoder, heads an engineer's train along the slow line as a pair of Bachmann 4-CEPs overtake a double headed oil train. The two Class 33s are fitted with Zimo MX645 decoders.

to Hornby RailMaster computer control software. To allow the full 56-point track diagram to be made available for operation, we set up a twin screen system connected to a PC tower using a pair of 27in monitors which displayed the complex trackplan in full in a similar style to what you might see in a railway power box. Following a few adjustments to point throw direction on the Saturday morning, it performed faultlessly throughout the weekend and in combination gave us a brilliant control system to keep the trains moving.

Throughout the weekend, our confidence with the layout grew and the new storage yard system also provided new route opportunities as well as a greater ability to create multiple train movements. At its height we had up to five trains on the move through the scenic section which was great to watch from the operator's position – we hope the visitors enjoyed the spectacle too.

Naturally, for its first showing in the new format, there were little niggles to address including reprogramming of one of the circuit breakers to suit its position as well as the addition of live wiring to a pair of sidings behind the scenes for the depot. We have also seen more potential for upgrades including some

potential changes to the trackplan for the scenic section for the 2018 show season to allow a more realistic flow of trains. We've also got new street lights to wire in, plans to introduce arc flashes at strategic points on the third-rail system with Train Tech products and a few other little details of this nature to make the scene around the railway come to life.

All in all, Twelve Trees' new format has been a great success and we are looking forward to taking it to the next level with the addition of the remaining 4ft of scenery at the station end of the layout. Initial plans include a gasometer, or two, as well as continuation of the street scene and possibly a new bridge across the station to allow the platforms to be extended to accommodate longer trains.

That is all in the future, but what is clear is that while we may have completed Twelve Trees' revival, this layout is far from complete. In fact, even on the rolling stock side alone there is enough to keep us busy for a long time to come. That though is the beauty of this layout. It will probably never be finished and we see it as being our flagship for the foreseeable future. Look out for future show dates in the pages of *Hornby Magazine* as we confirm its attendances for 2018 and beyond. ∎

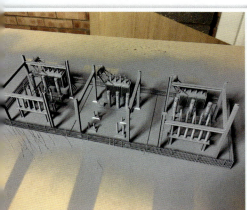

The Faller transformer station was built up and then painted with grey primer to more correctly resemble a British outline station. Detail painting followed.

It's October 3 and we are in the final stages of construction. The transformer station is being weighted down while its glue sets and the basics of ground cover are all in place.

A day later, and with 48 hours before the show opens, the third rail is installed and the ground cover is taking shape leaving final detailing, weathering and finishing tasks to be done.

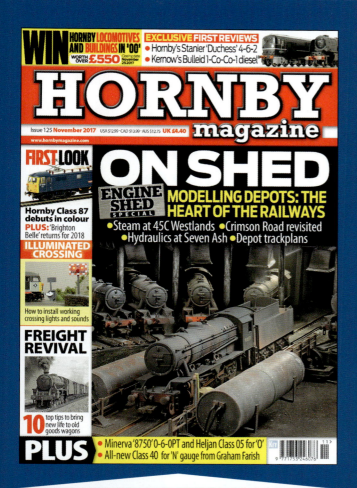
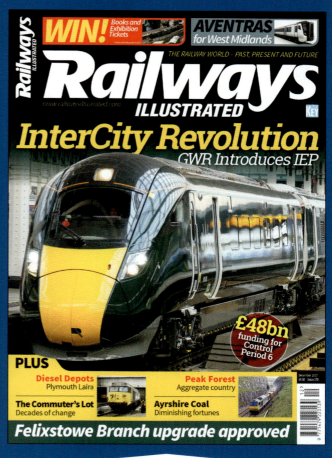

The Railfreight *Revolution*

TIM SHACKLETON customises a pair of 'OO' gauge Class 37s – one from Bachmann, the other from ViTrains – to mark 30 years of triple-grey Railfreight, one of the most striking liveries ever to adorn a UK freight locomotive.

I DON'T REMEMBER ANYTHING of the launch of the new Railfreight identity in a ceremony at Ripple Lane depot on October 15 1987. What I do recall with great clarity is the extraordinary storm that hit the United Kingdom that night. Woken by the din, I looked out of our bedroom window and saw in the eerie greyish light what appeared to be a river of debris flowing at great speed down the street – tree branches, roof tiles, dustbins. The power supply had failed, there were no lights on anywhere and for the next three days our village was cut off from the outside world.

When normality returned, so did my awareness of what had been going on at track level. In those days, I was heavily involved with high-end graphic design and the new sector liveries (from the Roundel Group, one of our main competitors in the corporate market) were hugely impressive – at least when first applied. Traditional BR drabness in the form of a triple-grey livery had been brilliantly countered by the imposition of colourful flashes and other graphics inspired, I'm told, by the markings on Polish Air Force jets.

Poking around the remains of Bedford shed one day, it was quite a shock to see a freshly repainted coal sector Class 56 swing under the bridge and on to the Bletchley line with a long line of immaculate yellow HAA hoppers, looking for all the world like something out of an advertising shoot (it possibly was). But within a few short years, the British climate had once again risen to the occasion and the combined effects of sun, wind, rain and snow had faded the sector markings and the subtly variegated greys into an all-purpose dinginess enhanced by liberal coatings of road dirt, soot and oil stains. By the early 1990s, to be frank, sector livery looked a mess and it was something of a mercy when the tired 'squadron' vinyls began to be removed from locomotives and in many cases replaced by the graphics of the new shadow privatisation companies – Mainline, LoadHaul and Transrail. Even at today's pace, seven years is a pretty short innings for a railway livery – plenty of locomotives were still in 1965-style BR blue when triple-grey Railfreight was first introduced and quite a few survived it.

This piece has a twofold objective – to celebrate what on paper was one of the best and most aesthetically pleasing liveries ever applied to a British freight locomotive (National Power blue is my all-time favourite, along with ARC mustard) and to show you how I went about presenting a pair of Railfreight '37s' in typical latter-day condition. Along the way I'll make some modifications to the as-bought products to emphasise some of their differences while playing down others. This is all part of the plan and, as ever, should yield a better and more accurate pair of models. ∎

A pair of Immingham's 'heavyweight' Class 37/7s looking like they mean business – Railfreight livery made a great sight when locomotives were kept clean but cleanliness inevitably degenerated as privatisation approached. 37713 is a Bachmann model while 37884 *Gartcosh* is the much under-rated ViTrains version. In terms of appearance, I'm not sure which of the two I prefer.

STEP BY STEP **DETAILING AND FINISHING RAILFREIGHT CLASS 37s**

1 My starting point was two immaculate locomotives in sector livery – Bachmann's 37514 with Railfreight Metals sub-branding and ViTrains 37421 *Stombidae* in Petroleum colours. Outwardly similar, there are a host of interesting detail differences between the two locomotives but I will need to correct some elements too.

2 Sourcing models at affordable prices – an art form in itself – enables me to commit more cash to high-end aftermarket components such as these. The quality of detailing products from suppliers such as Shawplan and Modelu goes way beyond the white metal blobs that were around a few years ago.

3 Adding the parts from the detailing pack can be a fiddle – the main problem is that the locating holes are invariably too small for the attaching lugs on the components. It's meant to be a push-fit but there are limits! To avoid damaging delicate details you can ease the holes slightly using either a drill bit or better still a tapered reamer – this will enable you to open out the hole just enough to push the parts home comfortably. A cautious dab of cyano doesn't go amiss to hold them in place.

4 Hornby offers an excellent set of front-end pipework for air-braked diesel classes, and I only wish it were available as a separate item. The Heljan and ViTrains equivalents are presentable but Bachmann's – apart from the screw couplings – are disappointing. I tend to make up my own bufferbeam detail from all kinds of sources – MJT vacuum pipes, Masokits screw couplings, leftovers, odd bits of wire. All are visible here and we still have some way to go.

5 If you're interested in minor detail variations, the '37's are a fabulous class to study. Many refurbished machines now only have one set of steps on the fuel tanks, under the access door at the fan end. For convenience, Bachmann and ViTrains give you the two each side with which they were originally built. I sliced off the moulded steps and – on the Bachmann model – infilled with 0.80in x 0.100in Evergreen styrene. The fuel gauge needs to go too.

6 The shortcomings of the various ready-to-run Class 37s have been endlessly discussed in print and online but the one thing that really sings out to me – the wildly inaccurate front windows – is hardly ever discussed. ViTrains' interpretation is the right size and shape but the glazing is too heavy. Bachmann's cab windows are too small and need work.

7 Here's a pair of modified 4mm scale Class 37s with accurate, flush-glazed front windows. As well as being the right size, these have the correct framing that represents the rubber gaskets. As per prototype, the whole assembly is set into a slightly raised panel that's not always visible in photographs.

8 This is where the problem lies. Once you pop the glazing out of the Bachmann version, the front end starts to look a lot better. It's clear that the manufacturer has included the prominent framing around each window as part of the clear plastic moulding. This has the effect of drastically reducing their apparent size.

9

Here's how I put it right. You can either flush-glaze the windows individually (as I'll do with the ViTrains model) or fit new etched window frames of the correct size. I still have some of the long-unavailable Craftsman Class 37 window etches (Extreme Etchings offers its own design). Having sprayed them satin black, they can be glazed with very thin material. I use 0.15mm mylar, from collectors' stamp packs, lightly glued with PVA.

10

A Class 37's front windows are raked back, so the frames need to be carefully bent to shape – it helps to cut a line clean through the glazing and lightly score the brass. Check the fit and then glue in place with tiny spots of cyano gel. All of a sudden, we have a Bachmann Class 37 that really looks like the real thing.

11

On the ViTrains 37 I used LaserGlaze windows from Brian Hanson at Shawplan. The originals aren't bad, but these are much better. The front end is the 'face' of a locomotive and anything that helps capture its essential character – such as replacement front windows – is a good thing.

12

Removing Bachmann's tampo-printed numbers is easy – I just scrape them off with my thumbnail (a wooden cocktail stick also works well). Any stubborn bits can then be carefully washed off with methylated spirits.

13

This is the outcome. Gentle abrasion doesn't seem to damage the paintwork beneath. The same is true of many Hornby models, making it easy to renumber them.

14

ViTrains graphics, on the other hand, seem impossible to shift without disturbing the underlying livery colour. In the end, I did what I could with a glass fibre burnishing brush and then undercoated the affected areas in white, finishing off with a top coat of Railmatch Executive Light Grey (200). This seemed a reasonable match with the colour ViTrains had chosen whereas the theoretically more accurate Rail Grey (206) didn't look right.

15

Unless the aim is to suggest a brand-new locomotive, we need to tone down the triple-grey Railfreight livery, suggesting the cumulative effects of wind and rain. There are various ways of doing this and my approach was to use a series of thin enamel washes. I began with MIG Ammo's panel line wash Pacific Dust (1604), applied with a half-inch flat brush.

Below: The photograph that inspired this whole project. In the heyday of sector liveries, 37713 emerges from Elland Tunnel with the 6E41 Blackburn to Lackenby steel empties on January 22 1992. It became the first class 37 to be repainted into Loadhaul livery in July 1994. Neil Harvey.

16

Modellers don't always seem to appreciate that, far from darkening, many liveries – grey particularly, but also yellow and blue – will lighten appreciably over time. Applying a fading effect will have the additional benefit of helping to even out the sometimes considerable variations in different manufacturers' interpretations of livery colours.

STEP BY STEP | DETAILING AND FINISHING RAILFREIGHT CLASS 37s

17

I continued to build up the effects using additional washes from the same range including Medium Tan (1606) and Tan Grey (1610). You need to allow a good 48 hours and preferably longer between applications for the oil-based paint to dry thoroughly, otherwise the colours will merge into one another. Who has that kind of patience? In the meantime, any rough edges (as on the yellow front ends) can be smoothed out.

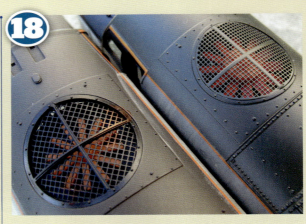

18

Bachmann's roof grille and fan (right) are fine but the ViTrains version needs attention. That undersized fan cuts no ice with me, while the grille mesh is coarse and incorrectly oriented.

19

20

I used a marker pen to pre-colour the fan detail. This saves having to paint and prime these delicate components. Once installed in the model, I'll add a light coat of weathering.

USEFUL LINKS	
Fox Transfers	www.fox-transfers.co.uk
Lifecolor	www.airbrushes.com
Markits	www.markits.com
MIG Ammo	www.migjimenez.com
Modelu	www.modelu3d.co.uk
Railmatch	www.howesmodels.co.uk
Shawplan/Extreme Etchings	www.shawplan.com

Once the pre-weathering faded effect had had time to dry, I removed the roof fan/grille assembly from the Vitrains model, ready for replacement with Extreme Etchings products from Brian Hanson. The air horns had already gone missing.

A Railfreight retrospective...

Below: When the going was good – 60095 *Crib Goch* arrives at Peak Forest on September 2 1994 with empty PHA wagons for the RMC quarries. Sector livery was designed with the Class 60s very much in mind and, with their slab sides and uncluttered front ends, they were easy to keep clean.

Above: Coal sector 56075 *West Yorkshire Enterprise* is a Hornby model with a lot of extra detail, mostly from Extreme Etchings. The weathering treatment is straightforward but note the use of artists' gouache to create subtle nuances of road dirt on the bodysides.

SKILL LEVEL
Beginner · Intermediate · Advanced

21 Markits' superb air horns are cross-drilled so they can be mounted on spikes of 0.45mm wire. I filled the overlarge holes with BlackTack – a high-strength adhesive putty that's like a much stronger version of BluTack. This provides a secure seating for the horns.

22 I can go on adding and modifying details almost indefinitely – here we have nameplates from Fox Transfers, crew figures from Modelu, yet more front-end pipework. Being very much a hands-on modeller I'm far more excited by a locomotive that needs a lot doing to it than one that's perfect straight out of the box.

23 Other than the roof and underframes, where I used an Iwata Revolution CS and LifeColor acrylics, there's hardly any airbrushing on these models. All the bodyside weathering is achieved with an initial application of enamel washes and the subsequent use of artists' oils, especially in the tumblehome area. Oil paints can be brushed on and washed off very easily using white spirit or turpentine.

Coal sector flashes didn't seem to fade as badly as some of the others. Class 37/3 37332 *The Coal Merchants Association of Scotland* is a Bachmann model given etched front windows. As per prototype, the horns have been repositioned on the bonnet tops.

37688 *Great Rocks* began life as a Lima model but has been heavily reworked. The weathering treatment – typical of the final days of Railfreight livery – involved a thin brown/grey mixture of enamel paints and then washing most of it off again with white spirit.

I described 37423 *Sir Murray Morrison* in the first of the two *Hornby Magazine* Skills Guides on weathering. I used faded Fox Transfers sector logos to convey the impression of rain and strong sunlight gradually toning down the paintwork. This is a ViTrains model with extra detail.

The end of the road for triple-grey Railfreight – in the final, bleak months of British Rail freight operations, Distribution-liveried 37238 and a de-branded split headcode Class 37 (still with its depot plaque) drag a container train from Felixstowe into Ipswich looking shabby beyond belief.

Upscaling

'O' gauge was once the preserve of the rich and skilled, but times are changing – and fast. **MIKE WILD** investigates the world of 7mm scale modelling and the rapidly increasing ready-to-run market.

FOR THE MAN ON THE STREET once there were only two real scale choices when it came to building a model railway – 'OO' or 'N' gauge. Both are well supported in the ready-to-run market and with a considerable backing from the cottage industries which provided every conceivable detail you could imagine. Prices are in line with our pockets and the availability of new products second to none in 'OO'.

'N' gauge has taken tremendous steps forward in the past decade and continues to do so with the latest revelation being the introduction of sound ready locomotives which are bringing a new dimension to the radically improved mechanicals of contemporary 'N'. The range of products is developing quickly

here too and we are seeing outdated models for iconic locomotives like the Stanier 'Duchess' and Collett 'Castle' replaced by up the minute highly detailed products.

However, there is a new choice which is being firmly offered up by increasing support from ready-to-run products and new technologies: 'O' gauge or 7mm:1ft scale if you prefer. This was once the preserve of the rich and skilled as you either needed plenty of money to support buying a ready made locomotive or serious ability to be able to turn flat sheets of etched brass into pinpoint accurate operating motive power and rolling stock. For many those two factors were great turn-offs together with the need for a substantial amount of space to build a layout, but at least now the tides are turning on the first two points.

Ready-to-run has always been a part of 'O' gauge with early coarse scale models from the tinplate era being the starting point. In more recent times we've seen an impressive array of high value hand assembled brass models from the likes of Loveless, Lee Marsh Models and Golden Age Models, all of which have produced absolutely stunning locomotive and carriage models, but at prices which the man on the street couldn't dream of affording. Still, no matter: they were aspirational and inspirational and it hasn't halted their progress or appeal with Loveless' product range including the prototype and production 'Deltics', LNER and LMS 'Pacifics', Lee Marsh the Stanier 'Princess', Fowler 'Patriot' and GWR '517' 0-4-2T and Golden Age LNER 'Pacifics', Bulleid 'Merchant Navys' and stunning Pullman cars to name but a few.

'O' gauge ready-to-run is developing and fast too. Not so long ago it was the preserve of the highly skilled, but with imposing locomotives like this Heljan Class 31 available off the shelf for less than £600 it is becoming more affordable and enticing too.

Hatton's is working with Heljan to produce a series of three LNER theme projects covering the Gresley 'A3' 4-6-2, as shown by this 3D printed sample, Gresley 'A4' 4-6-2 and three Gresley corridor carriages too.

Ready-to-run isn't confined to main manufacturers – Hatton's has stepped out to work directly with a factory in China to produce this new model of the 1942 introduced 'Warwell' wagon for 'O' gauge.

Affordable 'O'

The current revolution for 7mm scale can be traced back to 2005 when Danish manufacturer Heljan made its first move into ready-to-run locomotives at prices which, comparatively at least, were much more affordable.

Its first locomotive was the BR Western Region 'Hymek' which launched in 2005 with a sub-£400 price tag. It has never looked back, but initially development of the range was steady with on average one locomotive per year being planned. Then came Mk 1 carriages leading it into rolling stock while today it has an enviable back catalogue of 7mm scale diesel locomotives – classes 20, 25, 26, 31, 33, 37, 40, 42, 45, 47, 52, 53, 55 and 60 - most of which have only seen one production run, but still all within a maximum price of £700. That's still not

cheap by any stretch, but it is certainly more affordable.

Rising from Heljan's success in the market, we've seen more new names launch products including Ixion Models, which produced a Hudswell Clarke 0-6-0ST and Fowler 0-4-0 diesel shunter, Minerva Models which is developing its third ready-to-run steam locomotive and Dapol too, which is firmly established in the 'O' gauge market and now also owns the products produced by Lionheart Trains for the scale.

Most recently the Little Loco Company has sprung into the sector with its BTH Class 15 released in January 2017 and has three more projects on the go while Hatton's has

begun making inroads into the commission and exclusives market with four major projects for 'O' including Gresley 'A3' and 'A4' 4-6-2s priced at £750 each – a comparative brass built model would cost in the region of £2,500.

And the affordability isn't stuck at main line locomotives. Dapol's 'Terrier' and Class 08 both struck a chord with modellers of other scales – we know from conversations that many have bought these locomotives as display items as much as startup models - while its early 2017 release of BR built box and open wagons resulted in an immediate sell out to its retailers and the need to produce a second batch. At less than £45 per wagon, their prices were comparable with kits and, for the ready-to-run »

generation, met a higher standard of finish than the majority might be able to achieve by building their own.

Today's offerings

Each year we evaluate the range of ready-to-run locomotive models proposed for 'OO', 'N' and 'O' gauges and this year is no different – see Forward to 2018 on pages 120-127 – but looking back on this makes for fascinating reading. For 'O' gauge the number of planned locomotive projects on offer in 2016 doubled that of 2015 with nine steam and 11 diesels and now, at the end of 2017, we have a list of 20 locomotives, three carriages (from the same family) and six wagons to await – that's 29 items in total for a scale which was once considered a minority. And that follows the release of the 'Victory' 0-6-0T by Minerva, Class 08 by Dapol, Class 15 by Little Loco and Class 05, 37 and 45 by Heljan in the past 12 months. Add to that the Peckett 'E' 0-4-0ST from Minerva, Dapol's 'Terrier' and the Heljan 'Warship', *Falcon* and Class 25 in 2016 and it's a busy picture for 'O' gauge.

The breadth of the range is as impressive as the amount being offered. Heljan has

Laser cut buildings are becoming a popular choice for 'O' gauge not least because it allows small numbers of a high standard to be produced. This is the Intentio LNER platelayers hut which is simple to assemble.

upped its game considerably and has seen the light to move into both steam and DMU outline models. Meanwhile, newcomer Little Loco Company is making great strides into its

planned and yet to be announced projects with development of its Ruston 48DS running alongside a crowd-funded model of the Class 50 and development of an as yet publicly

unnamed Type 2 diesel. Minerva has been pushing along with its GWR '8750'/'57XX' 0-6-0PT project as a follow up to its Peckett 'E' 0-4-0ST and Kerr Stuart 'Victory' 0-6-0T with first of the the 'Panniers' arriving in late August covering the '8750' class.

Dapol has made big inroads into the small locomotives and rolling stock sector with its BR 12ton box vans and five plank open wagons going down a storm - and it has announced new salt and lime wagons too. Plus it is working through delivery of its own GWR '57XX'/'8750' 0-6-0PT and LMS 'Jinty' 0-6-0T for release in late 2017. It has also been making good use of its inherited Lionheart Trains product range to deliver GWR 'B-set' stock and 14ton Air Ministry four-wheel tankers which will soon be joined by new runs of '64XX' 0-6-0PTs, GWR Autocoaches and a new batch of GWR '45XX' 2-6-2Ts too.

Retailer Hatton's entering the 'O' gauge sector is perhaps one of the biggest surprises – and a good one too - with its 2016 announcement of the Gresley 'A3' and 'A4' 4-6-2s allied with a trio of Gresley teak corridor carriages – all produced through Heljan – together with its development of a model of

Heljan released this useful diesel depot kit in 2017 with a modular format which allows it to be extended and built with open and closed ends. It will surely inspire plenty of 'O' gauge depot scenes.

the LMS 'Warwell' bogie well wagon through its own sources. These four projects combined will open up new potential for the market and offer an impressive line of choices to this rapidly developing scale.

If all that isn't enough and you need more rolling stock in kit form, then Parkside Dundas, Slaters and Just Like the Real Thing are the places to start while for track the simplest entry point is Peco's range of bullhead and flat bottom rail which can be laid on Woodland Scenics sound deadening track underlay.

Away from the rails

Activity and development for 'O' gauge is far from limited to rail mounted vehicles – buildings, figures, structures and more are all being created and some with the assistance of new technologies too.

Heljan impressed in the first half of the year with release of its modular diesel depot kit, which can be built to any length to cover two roads and with either open or a combination of open and closed ends. In the summer Bachmann released a range of accessories for the scale consisting of locomotive lifting jacks, modern station details, lineside cabinets, coolant trolleys and a pair of platform tractor units. In addition a launch range of 12 figure packs have been released covering passengers, lineside workers and station staff – more are expected in the future.

If you are looking for road vehicles there is an increasing range of off-the-shelf products to supplement kits including products from Oxford Diecast and Corgi Collectables. These ➤➤

PLANNED 'O' GAUGE LOCOMOTIVES 2017-2018		
GWR '43XX' 2-6-0	Heljan	2018
GWR '61XX' 2-6-2T	Heljan	2018
GWR '14XX' 0-4-2T	Dapol	2018
GWR '8750'/'57XX' 0-6-0PT	Dapol	2018
LMS 'Jinty' 0-6-0T	Dapol	2017
LNER 'A3' 4-6-2	Hatton's/Heljan	2018
LNER 'A4' 4-6-2	Hatton's/Heljan	2018
Hunslet 'J94' 0-6-0ST	DJ Models	TBA
Ruston 48DS	Little Loco Company	2017
Class 03	Heljan	TBA
Class 20 (centre headcode)	Heljan	2017
Class 23	DJ Models	TBA
Class 25/3	Heljan	2018
Class 50	Heljan	2018
Class 50	Little Loco Company	2018
Class 117	Heljan	2018
Class 120	Heljan	2018
Class 121	Heljan	2018
Class 128	Heljan	2018

PLANNED 'O' GAUGE CARRIAGES 2017-2018		
LNER teak Corridor Third	Hatton's/Heljan	2018
LNER teak Open Third	Hatton's/Heljan	2018
LNER teak Brake Composite	Hatton's/Heljan	2018

PLANNED 'O' GAUGE WAGONS 2017-2018		
BR 20ton brake van	Dapol	2018
HAA hopper	Dapol	2018
HEA hopper	Dapol	2018
VEA vanwide	Dapol	2018
BR Meat van	Dapol	2017
Salt/lime wagons	Dapol	2018
LMS Warwell	Hatton's	2017

The Little Loco Co debuted its Class 15 in early 2017. Here it runs around *Hornby Magazine's* 'O' gauge test track with a trio of Dapol BR 10ft wheelbase wagons at the head of its goods. The retaining walls and platelayers hut are Intentio laser cut kits awaiting painting.

In 2017 Dapol took over the Lionheart Trains brand which includes locomotives, carriages and wagons for 'O' gauge. An attractive vehicle among the collection is this GWR autocoach which is a perfect partner for its GWR '64XX' 0-6-0PT.

Model Railway Wagons produces a range of magnetic couplings which can be used to introduce hands free coupling as well as reducing the strain of coupling screw link couplings between corridor carriages. This shows the Magclip couplings fitted to a pair of Heljan Mk 1s – installation takes around five minutes per vehicle end.

include both private and light commercials, although buses and lorries are few and far between in ready made format.

Buildings, accessories and detailing are well catered for by a wide range of companies, but there are a few that we will mention specifically here. These include ModelU which produces laser scanned and 3D printed figures with lifelike poses – these can even be modelled on yourself by visiting the ModelU stand at exhibitions – while Skytrex offers an impressive catalogue of lineside furniture, buildings, structures and walling made from resin.

For something to really make your layout stand out, the new Intentio range of laser cut building kits and structures is well worth investigating. Their detailing is exquisite as we have found with the retaining wall sections which we have been installing on *Hornby Magazine's* office test track to assess its future development.

Also well worth a look is Model Railway Wagons which offers a superb magnetic coupling system perfect for use with Heljan Mk 1 carriages and other vehicles as well as a substantial range of etched brass kits while the Gauge O Guild is a valuable resource of information on all matters 7mm scale.

The Dapol Class 08, released in the final weeks of 2016, has been an instant hit both with modellers and collectors alike.

Modern wonders

The advent of modern ready-to-run mass produced models is doing wonders for the potential of 'O' gauge and opening up the scale to a section of the market which could once only aspire to its gripping potential. The size of the locomotives is a joy to behold and finally we are seeing a buoyant market which is set to inspire new generations of larger scale modellers. Great news for all. ■

USEFUL LINKS	
Skytrex	www.ogauge.co.uk
Tower Models	www.tower-models.com
Heljan	www.heljan.dk
Little Loco Company	www.littleloco.co.uk
Dapol	www.dapol.co.uk
Minerva Model Railways	www.minervamodelrailways.co.uk
Hatton's	www.hattons.co.uk
Intentio	www.intentio.co.uk
ModelU	www.modelu3d.co.uk
Bachmann	www.bachmann.co.uk
Parkside Models	www.peco-uk.com
KS Laser Designs	www.kslaserdesigns.com
Slaters	www.slatersplastikard.com
Just Like the Real Thing	www.justliketherealthing.co.uk
Gauge O Guild	www.gauge0guild.com

Dapol is making great strides into the 'O' gauge market and appears to be clearly focused on producing smaller and affordable locomotives. This is the decorated sample of its new LMS Fowler 'Jinty' 0-6-0T which was released in the early October 2017 as a follow up to its highly popular 'Terrier' and Class 08 for the scale.

Heljan's move into 'O' gauge steam locomotives has started with a pair of GWR locomotives including this model of the Churchward '43XX' 2-6-0 which is due for release in 2018.

Review of the Year
2016-2017

The past 12 months have delivered an exciting range of new releases from the smallest shunting engines to the largest 'Pacifics'. **MIKE WILD** reviews 2017's debuts for 'OO', 'O' and 'N' gauge.

I T'S BEEN A YEAR OF CONTRASTS with an incredible range of new locomotives, carriages and wagons touching down from an increasing number of manufacturers. In total 60 promised new products have been released and there are more on the water from China as I type.

Model railway production and delivery has never been so intense and nor have there been so many names in the game. What was once the preserve of Hornby, Bachmann, Dapol and Heljan just a few years ago now includes

names as diverse as Kernow Model Rail Centre, Hatton's, Realtrack Models, Revolution Trains, Rapido, Minerva Model Railways and the Little Loco Company. It is clear that ready-to-run is gaining more ground each year and providing an ever more wide ranging selection of items to choose from and the standards of detail and value are also being challenged too.

Most interesting in 2017 is the trade of places between 'N' and 'O' gauge. During the past year, 'N' gauge has taken something of a back seat in comparison with its larger cousin with just four newly tooled models arriving during

the year by the time this Yearbook closed for press. Naturally there have been reliveries and renumbering of existing items, but here we are solely focused on models which made their first appearance this year.

On the other hand, 'O' gauge is going from strength to strength in the ready-to-run sector and attracting a new level of interest from modellers and manufacturers. The latest name to join the 'O' gauge portfolio is the Little Loco Company, which debuted its Class 15 Bo-Bo Type 1 diesel in January 2017. It is already working on its follow up – the Ruston 48DS

Kernow Model Rail Centre's new 'OO' gauge model of the Bulleid designed 1-Co-Co-1 offers a stunning replica of these popular prototypes.

Kernow Model Rail Centre had a busy year with its fine model of the GWR '1361' 0-6-0ST being due to arrive in November alongside the Bulleid diesel and LSWR 'Gate stock'.

A collection of five new LNER Thompson corridor carriages were delivered by Bachmann for 'OO' with LNER faux teak versions to follow later this year.

4w diesel shunter – as well as supporting production of a Class 50 for the scale. This new name is bringing model railway production back to British soil too while Dapol has also invested in new equipment for its UK factory in Chirk to allow more products to be made in house without relying on China.

As you would expect, 'OO' is still the centre of attention when it comes to new releases with an impressive 43 brand new items being delivered since November 2016 when we signed off on Yearbook No. 10. That extends to 21 locomotives, 11 carriages and 11 goods wagons too – impressive indeed and plenty to keep our wallets open on a regular basis too!

Industrial delight

With so much to choose from – and a whole host of reliveried and renumbered models too numerous to list here – there was one model of all those listed here which stole the model railway world's attention more than any other: Hornby's Peckett 'W4' 0-4-0ST. This tiny locomotive sold out before it had even reached the shops and has certainly garnered a lot of attention for the potential of small industrial locomotives in 'OO' gauge.

In fact, small locomotives were a common theme during the year with Heljan releasing its promised models of the GWR '1361' 0-6-0ST and '1366' 0-6-0PT, Kernow Model Rail Centre (KMRC) its GWR '1361' 0-6-0ST, Golden Valley Hobbies the Yorkshire Engine Co 'Janus' 0-6-0 diesel shunter and Hatton's the GWR '14XX' 0-4-2T family, all in 'OO' gauge. And who could forget Bachmann's Wickham Type 27 engineers trolley which arrived in the shops in November 2016?

This trend for compact motive power was supported further with Hatton's announcement of the South Eastern & Chatham Railway Wainwright 'P' 0-6-0T and Andrew Barclay industrial 0-4-0ST in September for the release in December 2017 and January 2018 respectively.

It wasn't just 'OO' that benefitted from new small shunting locomotives either with

Hornby extended its BR Mk 1 portfolio with the Brake Second Open and First Open vehicles in 'OO'.

'O' gauge receiving its fair share too. Top of the list was Dapol's Class 08 diesel shunter – a long time coming, but well worth the wait – which was followed almost immediately by Minerva's second ready-to-run product for the scale in the Kerr, Stuart 'Victory' 0-6-0T a month later. Fast forward to the end of the summer and two more six-coupled locomotives arrived in the shape of Minerva's GWR '8750' 0-6-0PT and Heljan's Hunslet Class 05 diesel shunter which was followed by the the LMS Fowler 'Jinty' 0-6-0T by Dapol in the first weeks of October.

Main line motive power

Hornby led the charge for main line motive power in 'OO' gauge with its models of the LNER 'B12' 4-6-0 and, more importantly, the big 'missing link' in the 'Pacific' portfolio: Bulleid's air-smoothed 'Merchant Navy' 4-6-2 covering all the build series and variations. Its all new model of the Stanier 'Duchess' was just days away from arrival in the UK too in October.

Bachmann wasn't out of the picture as it delivered the long-awaited model of the LMS Stanier 'Mogul' as well as the London & North Western Railway Webb 'Coal Tank' 0-6-2T for Midland Region modellers of the steam era. Bachmann's Graham Farish brand also delivered 'N' gauge's sole new steam locomotive of 2017: the GWR 'Castle' 4-6-0 which also became the first in its range to be fitted with a Next18 decoder socket and the first British outline factory fitted sound steam locomotive for 'N'. It was followed in October by the first of the new 'N' gauge Class 40s.

Interestingly, despite the comprehensive range of diesel and electric locomotives and units already available, 2017 saw some significant new arrivals for this sector. Highlights included the Vossloh Class 68 Bo-Bo diesel from Dapol as well as a first for the UK market with DJ Models delivering its Class 71 which, following in the footsteps of Hornby's well received 2016 model of the same class, became Britain's premier crowd-funded ready-to-run 'OO' gauge locomotive.

Multiple units were in focus with four new options coming to the fore. Headed by

Heljan focused on smaller locomotives for 'OO' in 2017 including the attractive GWR '1366' 0-6-0PT.

Dapol's Class 122, this attractive single car Gloucester Diesel Multiple Unit (DMU) was soon followed by KMRC's impressive 4-TC four-car trailer control unit for the Southern Region, Bachmann's Class 450 'Desiro' for the modern

day third-rail network and finally Realtrack Models' Class 156 two-car DMU. The new Class 156 is stunning and arguably the finest ready-to-run DMU we have seen yet – a bold claim, but one which few would refute.

However, one of the most enticing items came in just a few weeks before we closed for press as the first full production version of Kernow Model Rail Centre's model of Bulleid prototype diesel 10201 touched down in mid-September. This eye-catching 1-Co-Co-1 was first announced by Kernow in 2010 and has taken a long time to develop, but there is no doubting that the wait has been worth it. The full production batch was being shipped in September and expected to arrive with Kernow in late October/early November, modelling locomotives 10201 and 10202. The third, and quite different, engine 10203 is also on the cards for later release.

Veterans lead the way

Passenger stock has always been an important part of the ready-to-run market, but in the past decade, standards of detail have advanced immensely and we are now also seeing vehicle designs which were once purely the pursuit of experienced kit builders.

The highlight of 2017's carriage releases were Bachmann's trio of SECR 'Birdcage' vehicles which, although at the top end of the price spectrum, offered a venerable design which

DJ Models scored a first for 'OO' gauge – its Class 71 being the first crowd-funded locomotive model to be delivered for the scale.

"Hornby led the charge for main line motive power in 'OO' gauge."

MIKE WILD

Minerva's third 'O' gauge locomotive was this model of the GWR '8750' 0-6-0PT which was set to be followed soon after by the '57XX'.

will stand out on any Southern Railway/Region layout for their unique design. The 'Birdcage' name was derived from the raised guard's lookout on the brake coaches and they were usually marshalled into three-car sets with a brake at each end.

Bachmann produced three unique vehicles for its collection consisting of the Brake Third, Brake Third Lavatory and Lavatory Composite. The first set to arrive were delivered in BR crimson and these were to be followed by SECR dark lake and Southern Railway liveries.

Also arriving in the *Hornby Magazine* office in September were production versions of Kernow Model Rail Centre's London & South Western

The Oxford Rail 'Carflat' provides an unusual but versatile vehicle for passenger and goods formations in 'OO'.

Dapol delivered its Class 122 Gloucester RCW railcar for 'OO' in the middle of the year.

Railway 'Gate stock'. These two-car push-pull sets were announced as a partner to the Cornish retailer's 2016 released Adams 'O2' 0-4-4T and model the 1914-introduced

carriages. Part of the fleet remained in service into the early 1960s and Kernow is producing versions in Southern Railway and BR liveries.

The most modern carriages to be produced for 'OO' during 2017 were Bachmann's collection of five Thompson steel panelled corridor stock and Hornby's new additions to its BR Mk 1 carriage range.

The Thompsons debuted in BR carmine and cream livery in February 2017 covering five different vehicle types while a follow up batch in 'faux teak' were expected to be released in December 2017/January 2018 following a number of revisions to the artwork for the complex decoration of these vehicles.

Hornby's new Mk 1s covered the Brake Second Open – the first time an accurate model of this vehicle type has been produced for 'OO' – and the First Open which were made available in BR blue and grey (October 2017) and BR maroon liveries (planned for release in November 2017).

Away from 'OO', Great Western Railway carriage designs were in focus with Graham Farish releasing its 'N' gauge Hawksworth 'Autocoach', to complement its 2016 model of

the GWR '64XX' 0-6-0PT, while Dapol delivered the GWR 'B-set' brakes for 'O' gauge completing a model started by Lionheart Trains which is now under the Dapol umbrella.

Wagons roll

Goods stock has been a strong focus of the year with 10 new vehicles landing for 'OO', one for 'N' and a group of five for 'O' gauge.

Our review period starts with the arrival of Hornby's LMS 20ton coke hopper and Southern Railway cattle wagons for 'OO', both of which were announced for its 2016 catalogue launch. Each delivered an impressive level of detail and saw introduction of new split spoke design wheels for Hornby's freight stock.

However, Hornby also made sure that its first all-new 2017 range goods wagon – the GWR diagram AA15 20ton 'Toad' brake van – was delivered promptly with the first two versions touching down in August. These brand new items delivered a superb model which included separately fitted handrails throughout and a highly detailed moulded body which catered for original planked and later modified vans with steel plating to the lower panels.

Hornby delivered its brand new Stanier 'Duchess' 4-6-2 just in time to make this year's Yearbook. This is its model of 46256 Sir William A Stanier FRS in BR lined maroon - one of the two Ivatt modified locomotives.

Bachmann's long awaited 'OO' model of the LMS Stanier 'Mogul' was an instant hit. This is the LMS lined black version as 2965.

Heljan brought new opportunities for 1960s block fuel/oil trains in February and March with the arrival, first, of its 35ton Class B four-wheel oil tanker and then the similar 35ton Class A four-wheel petrol tanker. Both versions offered a range of livery options and allow prototypical block formations to be created for the final years of steam through to the 1970s.

One wagon design became the source of two ready-to-run models: the 1942 introduced LMS 'Warwell' bogie well wagon. These were built

Heljan's 'O' gauge Class 37 with centre headcodes was a rapid sell out on arrival and a second batch in large logo blue was produced in the early autumn.

primarily for the movement of tanks in support of the Second World War and following on from Hatton's revealing its project to develop models in 'OO' and 'O' gauge in 2016 Oxford Rail announced that it was working on the same vehicle for 'OO' at its 2017 range launch in January.

It became a race to the finish for 'OO' and Hatton's got its vehicles out a few weeks before Oxford. The major difference between the two is weight – Hatton's version featuring a die-cast chassis for increased track force as well as 10 different liveries straight off the blocks including early and late wagons, track panel carriers and rail carriers. Oxford has been working through its schedule of 'Warwells' with early versions coming through first - one with a Sherman tank - and most recently a BR bauxite model.

Also delivered by Oxford was its 2016 announced BR 57ft 'Carflat'. This useful vehicle, which can be operated with passenger stock, in mixed goods formations or in block formations, has been made available in BR maroon and BR blue schemes and concurrently Oxford Rail released four-packs of cars to suit different periods of operation to load the flats.

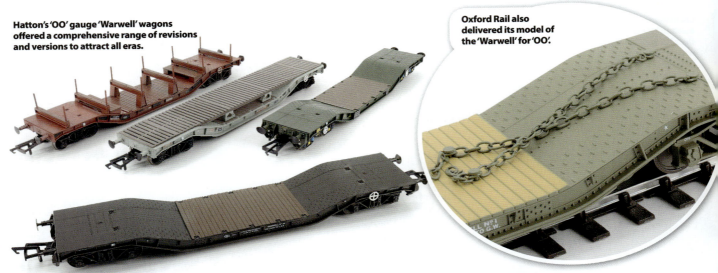

Hatton's 'OO' gauge 'Warwell' wagons offered a comprehensive range of revisions and versions to attract all eras.

Oxford Rail also delivered its model of the 'Warwell' for 'OO'.

The modern modeller wasn't quite so well served with freight stock this year, but it did see the release of Dapol's MJA Freightliner bogie twin-set box wagons together with Kernow Model Rail Centre's PBA 'Clay Tiger' bogie covered hopper to provide new choices for diesel traction to haul.

In 'N' gauge it was DJ Model's 'Mermaid' ballast tippler which saved the day for freight stock while in 'O' gauge Dapol struck gold with the release of its collection of BR 10ft

wheelbase wagons covering planked and plywood sided 12ton vent vans, an insulated 10ton van, five-plank open wagon and, most recently, the BR 10ton meat van. All used the same chassis and the first batch was an instant sell out leading to a second production run being authorised by the manufacturer.

The best of...

With so many outstanding product choices coming through, picking the best is a near impossible task. We'll all have our own views – in fact, personal leanings within the *Hornby Magazine* office have seen differences of opinion between steam and modern traction already. That said, there are clearly models

In 'O' gauge Heljan's Class 45 1-Co-Co-1 captured much attention for its size and quality too.

Modern day Southern Region modellers were treated to the arrival of Bachmann's 'OO' model of the Class 450 'Desiro'.

which stand out above the others such as Hornby's Peckett 0-4-0ST and Realtrack Models' Class 156 for 'OO' - and who could fail to notice the impact of Little Loco Co's Class 15 and Dapol's 10ft wheelbase wagons for 'O' gauge?

If you are looking for something truly different from the rest, then the pick of the bunch almost definitely has to be Kernow Model Rail Centre's model of Bulleid diesel 10201. This is its first model produced direct with the factory and, so far, this has to be a firm favourite of the year with the *Hornby Magazine* team. However, there is more to come with Hornby's enticing model of the SECR Wainwright 'H' 0-4-4T just weeks away as this Yearbook closed for press and the stunning all-new Stanier 'Duchess' which, we can firmly state, is even better in the flesh than it looks in photographs is due to arrive in the shops during October. You will be impressed by it for sure, but – as they say, that is another story. ∎

TABLE 1 - 2016-2017 NEW READY-TO-RUN PRODUCTS				
MODEL	**SCALE**	**MANUFACTURER**	**RELEASED**	**FEATURED**
LNER 'B12' 4-6-0	'OO'	Hornby	November 2016	HM114
Wickham Type 27 trolley and trailer	'OO'	Bachmann	November 2016	HM114
LNER 'A4' 4-6-2 (Black Label)	'OO'	Dapol	November 2016	HM114
Peckett 'W4' 0-4-0ST	'OO'	Hornby	December 2016	HM115
BR Class 08 0-6-0	'O'	Dapol	December 2016	HM115
SR 'Merchant Navy' 4-6-2	'OO'	Hornby	March 2017	HM116
LMS 20ton coke hopper	'OO'	Hornby	January 2017	HM116
SR 10ton cattle wagon	'OO'	Hornby	January 2017	
GWR '14XX' 0-4-2T	'OO'	Hattons	January 2017	HM116
Kerr, Stuart 'Victory' 0-6-0T	'O'	Minerva	January 2017	HM116
GWR '1366' 0-6-0PT	'OO'	Heljan	January 2017	HM117
BR 12ton planked box van	'O'	Dapol	January 2017	HM117
BR 12ton plywood box van	'O'	Dapol	January 2017	HM117
BR 10ton insulated box vans	'O'	Dapol	January 2017	HM117
BR five-plank open wagon	'O'	Dapol	January 2017	HM117
LMS Stanier 'Mogul' 2-6-0	'OO'	Bachmann	February 2017	HM117
LNER Thompson Corridor First	'OO'	Bachmann	February 2017	HM117
LNER Thompson Corridor Third	'OO'	Bachmann	February 2017	HM117
LNER Thompson Corridor Composite	'OO'	Bachmann	February 2017	HM117
LNER Thompson Brake Composite	'OO'	Bachmann	February 2017	HM117
LNER Thompson Brake Third	'OO'	Bachmann	February 2017	HM117
BR Class 15 Bo-Bo	'O'	Little Loco	January 2017	HM117
Vossloh Class 68 Bo-Bo	'OO'	Dapol	February 2017	HM118
GWR '1361' 0-6-0ST	'OO'	Heljan	February 2017	HM118
Class B 35ton oil tanker	'OO'	Heljan	February 2017	HM118
Class A 35ton oil tanker	'OO'	Heljan	March 2017	
GWR Hawksworth Autocoach	'N'	Graham Farish	March 2017	HM118
LNWR 'Coal Tank' 0-6-2T	'OO'	Bachmann	April 2017	HM119
Freightliner MJA box wagon twin-set	'OO'	Dapol	April 2017	HM119
GWR 'Castle' 4-6-0	'N'	Graham Farish	April 2017	HM119
BR Class 37 Co-Co	'O'	Heljan	March 2017	HM119
BR Class 45 1-Co-Co-1	'O'	Heljan	April 2017	HM120
BR Class 122 DMU	'OO'	Dapol	May 2017	HM121
BR 'Mermaid' ballast tippler	'N'	DJ Models	May 2017	HM121
BR Class 71 Bo-Bo	'OO'	DJ Models	May 2017	HM121
PBA 'Clay Tiger' bogie hopper	'OO'	Kernow	May 2017	HM121
GWR 'B-set' brakes	'O'	Dapol	May 2017	
IDA 'Super Low' container wagons	'OO'	Dapol	June 2017	
GWR 'Dean Goods' 0-6-0	'OO'	Oxford Rail	June 2017	HM122
'Warwell' bogie well wagon	'OO'	Hattons	June 2017	HM122
BR 57ft 'Carflat'	'OO'	Oxford Rail	June 2017	HM122
YEC 'Janus' 0-6-0 diesel shunter	'OO'	Golden Valley	June 2017	HM122
BR 4-TC four-car trailer-control unit	'OO'	Kernow	September 2017	HM123
Class 450 'Desiro' four-car unit	'OO'	Bachmann	September 2017	HM123
GWR 'Toad' 20ton brake van	'OO'	Hornby	August 2017	HM123
'Warwell' bogie well wagon	'OO'	Oxford Rail	August 2017	HM123
BR Class 156 two-car DMU	'OO'	Realtrack Models	August 2017	HM124
BR Mk 1 Brake Second Open	'OO'	Hornby	October 2017	HM124
SECR 'Birdcage' Brake Third	'OO'	Bachmann	October 2017	HM124
SECR 'Birdcage' Composite Lavatory	'OO'	Bachmann	October 2017	HM124
SECR 'Birdcage' Brake Lavatory	'OO'	Bachmann	October 2017	HM124
GWR '1361' 0-6-0ST	'OO'	Kernow	November 2017	HM124
GWR '8750' 0-6-0PT	'O'	Minerva	August 2017	HM125
BR 12ton meat vans	'O'	Dapol	August 2017	
Bulleid 1-Co-Co-1	'OO'	Kernow	November 2017	HM125
LSWR 'Gate stock' push-pull set	'OO'	Kernow	November 2017	HM125
BR Mk 1 First Open	'OO'	Hornby	October 2017	HM125
BR Class 05 0-6-0 diesel shunter	'O'	Heljan	September 2017	HM125
LMS Stanier 'Duchess' 4-6-2	'OO'	Hornby	October 2017	HM125
BR Class 40 1-Co-Co-1 diesel	'N'	Graham Farish	October 2017	HM125

Golden Valley Hobbies worked with Oxford Rail to develop this 'OO' gauge YEC 'Janus' 0-6-0.

'Motorail'

INCREASED OWNERSHIP of motor cars in the 1950s meant more freedom to travel where you wanted, when you wanted, but long-distance journeys could still be slow tortuous affairs, especially during the summer months. Pinch points combined with additional traffic on holiday routes throughout the UK, particularly the West Country and Scotland, could add much time to a journey. Bypasses and dual-carriageways were in their infancy, and Britain's first motorway only opened towards the end of the decade.

British Railways (BR) recognised this, introducing a new domestic car-carrying service between London and Scotland in the mid-1950s with its 'Car Sleeper Limited', comprising 11 Covered Carriage Trucks (CCTs), three sleeping cars and three seated vehicles. It was booked to depart London King's Cross early evening, with passengers retiring to their sleeper berths having loaded their vehicles into the car-carrying vans and waking up refreshed the following morning at Perth – the journey taking approximately ten hours. A daytime service, the 'Anglo-Scottish Car Carrier', followed, operating between London Holloway Road and Newcastle/Edinburgh, and car loading facilities were added at selected stations on the Eastern and North Eastern Regions, promoting the ability to transport your vehicle between any two of these locations, while new longer distance services began to appear between other principal towns and cities.

By the early 1960s, operations had expanded to such an extent that car-carrying services could be found radiating to/from Eastbourne, Edinburgh, Exeter, Glasgow, Inverness, Newcastle, Newhaven, Newton Abbot, Okehampton, Penzance, St Austell, Stirling, Surbiton, Sutton Coldfield, York and more. Incidentally, many of these trains ran on specific days of the week or at certain times of the year, such as BR Southern Region's distinctive 'Surbiton to Okehampton Car Carrier', formed of up to eight BR Mk 1 GUVs and three seated vehicles.

Whilst initially operating under the car-carrying service banner, in the mid-1960s the business was rebranded 'Motorail' and encompassed all passenger car-carrying services. Despite improved motorway networks during the 1970s and 1980s helping to reduce road journey times, 'Motorail' services still took in a vast array of destinations including Aberdeen, Bristol, Brockenhurst, Cambridge, Carlisle, Carmarthen, Crewe, Dover, Edinburgh, Ely, Fishguard, Harwich, Inverness, Newton Abbot, Newton-Le-Willows, Penzance, Perth, Plymouth, Reading, Sheffield, Stirling, Sutton Coldfield, Totnes, York and more.

However, by the 1990s the writing was on the wall, with just a handful of services operating as part of the overnight sleeper train network to Aberdeen, Edinburgh, Fort William, Glasgow and Inverness, with operation coming to an end

trains

For two decades, 'Motorail' trains helped motorists avoid traffic jams until the widespread opening of the motorway network. **MARK CHIVERS** examines their introduction, operation and eventual decline.

in the mid-1990s. For a brief spell from 1999, 'Motorail' was resurrected by First Great Western on a limited basis between London and the West Country, formed of newly-converted rolling stock which enabled vehicles to be loaded and off-loaded directly via the platform, but this also came to an end in the mid-2000s.

Rolling Stock

Initially, older rolling stock was converted for use on car-carrying services, but in due course new bespoke vehicles appeared, including the unique BR Mk 1 two-tier car transporter vans (TCVs) built by Newton Chambers in the early 1960s and used on services to Scotland and the West Country.

A new fleet of BR Mk 1 four-wheel CCT vans was also built, although they were subsequently deemed unsuitable for use on 'Motorail' services due to their restricted top speed, while its roster of car-carrying BR Mk 1 57ft bogie General Utility Vans (GUVs) proved altogether more successful.

In the mid-1960s, Rootes/Pressed Steel were contracted to build a small fleet of CARTIC-4 two-tier articulated car-carrying sets. Each set comprised four vehicles running on articulated bogies and were utilised on a variety of services, until eventually being absorbed into freight stock for use on commercial car-carrying services. The 1960s also saw a large number of pre-nationalisation and BR Mk 1 carriage underframes converted to bogie Carflat wagons.

This fleet of Carflats incorporated examples in freight service for commercial automotive traffic, as well as those used for domestic car-carrying services. To differentiate the freight vehicles from 'Motorail' examples, those allocated to passenger services were subsequently painted blue and carried 'Motorail' legends on boards mounted to the side stanchions. BR bauxite painted examples were utilised on freight traffic and would often be seen in block trains of new car/van deliveries heading from manufacturing plants to distribution points around the country, as well as

the occasional mixed freight formation too.

At the height of its popularity, 'Motorail' passenger accommodation was mainly formed of BR Mk 1 or Mk 2 carriages, with customers offered a mix of onward travel either by combined daytime 'Motorail' services, combined overnight sleeper services or by timetabled passenger train, with cars travelling separately on a train formed purely of car-carrying vehicles. The combined services could be very long once seated and sleeper vehicles together with nine or more bogie Carflats were added.

By the late 1980s, the bogie Carflat vehicles and two-tier car carriers had been withdrawn and replaced by BR Mk 1 57ft GUVs. As new stock and methods of operation were introduced, the Mk 1 GUVs also operated with air-conditioned BR Mk 2d-f and Mk 3 locomotive-hauled coaching stock. Amongst the anomalies were InterCity's West Coast Main Line Anglo-Scottish services on which you might witness a rake of BR Mk 3 carriages top-and-tailed with a Mk 3 Driving Van »

Bulleid 'West Country' 34036 *Westward Ho* **leads the Surbiton-Okehampton car carrier through Twelve Trees Junction representing the formation in the early 1960s. The Mk 1 GUV vans are special commissions on the Bachmann model by Kernow Model Rail Centre.**

Trailer (DVT) at the front and a Class 87 electric locomotive to the rear, together with four or five BR Mk 1 'Motorail' GUVs tacked on behind the locomotive, making for a strange sight.

Notably, many of the daytime 'Motorail' services appear to have included mainly First Class accommodation, with some offering onboard buffet/restaurant facilities. For those services without catering, it was possible to book refreshments and food in advance. Overnight 'Motorail' operations usually offered a selection of First and Second class seated and sleeper accommodation, although this was quite limited on some trains such as the Brockenhurst to Stirling service which could be formed of two BR Mk 1 Sleeper Seconds (SLS/SLSTP), a Corridor First (FK) and Brake Open Second (BSO) together with up to six Carflats for part of the journey.

In the final years of BR's 'Motorail' operations in the mid-1990s, services concentrated primarily on the Anglo-Scottish routes and were amongst the longest trains to operate on BR at the time, with the service bound for the Highlands splitting into smaller portions at Edinburgh to/from Aberdeen, Fort William and Inverness. As an example, the Fort William train could be formed with a Class 37/4 diesel hauling an air-conditioned Mk 2 BSO, three Mk 3 sleepers (SLE/SLEP) and three BR Mk 1 GUVs.

Operations

While carrying cars by rail was not a new phenomenon to the railway, the ability to load vehicles at railway stations, as opposed to goods yards or manufacturing plants, required new facilities to be installed.

At their most basic, this could be a wooden or metal ramp placed over a buffer stop, with examples at Brockenhurst, Inverness and St Austell or even a bespoke ramp constructed at the end of a siding close to the station such as at Fort William and Sutton Coldfield. Where goods yards already had a loading/unloading facility, such as the military sidings at Okehampton, these were utilised for the car-carrying trains that operated to and from the station too.

Some facilities were more dependent on the stock deployed and might require more specialist equipment to be installed, such as the metal ramp construction used at the Caledonian Road loading point in North London for use with the BR Mk 1 two-tier Car Transporter Vans (TCV), which required vehicles to be loaded at a higher level, as two cars per van were then subsequently lowered by hydraulic lift to sit between the bogies while four others were secured along the upper level. Similar higher-level loading facilities were required at terminals served by these vehicles, as well as providing more traditional loading methods for other vehicles. This makes for interesting modelling opportunities.

Where end-ramp facilities weren't available, some stations would utilise a side access ramp to enable vehicles to be loaded and off-loaded via the platform, while some stations such as Carlisle and London Euston utilised converted side-loading ramp wagons for a time which

enabled BR Mk 1 'Motorail' GUVs to be loaded/unloaded directly onto a platform. These were often marshalled to and from the main train by a Class 08 diesel shunter.

At Kensington Olympia in West London, a dedicated four-platform 'Motorail' facility was developed, acting as a hub for many services to/from and via London. Vehicles could be loaded directly onto the 'Motorail' Carflats or CARTIC-4 sets from the ramps at the reception end of the platform, with passenger carriages already attached at the front or remarshalled from the main station platforms. For example, a terminating lengthy mixed daytime train could arrive from the West Country and terminate in one of the long platforms, where the train locomotive would uncouple and run-round the formation, dropping onto the rear. Once the 'Motorail' vehicles had been uncoupled, the locomotive would then shunt them into one of the four loading/unloading bays. With unloading completed, the 'Motorail' vehicles would then be returned to the main train, re-attached and the whole formation removed for stabling. Some 'Motorail' services were also routed via Kensington Olympia to enable them to be split or combined for their onward journey.

On arrival, customers would check in at the 'Motorail' reception ahead of their car being loaded. Facilities were often limited, with some reception facilities resembling little more than a pre-fabricated building mounted on concrete blocks, presenting a somewhat temporary nature to the business. At larger sites, such as

At Darlington Brush Type 4 D1501 heads the down Anglo-Scottish car carrier on June 19 1967 formed of four Mk 1 passenger vehicles and six Mk 1 TCV twin deck car carriers. *Chris Davies/Railphotoprints.co.uk.*

the Kensington Olympia 'Motorail' Terminal which handled multiple arrivals and departures, dedicated signage would direct you to the correct train to ensure your vehicle ended up at the correct destination. The logistics of getting this right every time at all sites must have been immense.

For a time, special blue protective screens were also fitted over exposed car windscreens on vehicles carried by bogie Carflat and articulated CARTIC-4 wagons to reduce any potential damage during the journey. Depending on the location and stock used, on arrival at the train's destination wagons would usually be uncoupled and shunted to the 'Motorail' siding or platform for off-loading.

Some locations were fairly compact, such as St Austell in the West Country which comprised a couple of sidings alongside the station set within a concrete apron – one siding for Carflats, the other for carriage stabling, which involved meticulous shunting operations. At sites where side-loading was required, a ramp would be used to facilitate the loading/off-loading process at the platform. Loading gauges were also usually positioned at these points too, to ensure vehicles would not strike lineside structures such as platform awnings or bridges.

Although British Rail's 'Motorail' services ended more than two decades ago, there are still telltale signs dotted around the network. Keep your eyes peeled for the platform end loading ramps or rail-connected loading bays still in existence.

Models

From a modelling perspective, a good selection of suitable 'OO' gauge motive power is available

from the main manufacturers such as Bulleid 'Merchant Navy' 4-6-2s, Stanier 'Black Five' 4-6-0s, Gresley 'A4' 4-6-2s and BR 'Britannia' 4-6-2s together with the new order comprising Classes 08, 33, 37, 40, 42, 46, 47, 50 and 52 diesels too. However, suitable rolling stock is a little more difficult to come by, as some of the earlier more esoteric car-carrying vehicles are either only available in kit form or not at all.

That said, this year has seen a big gap plugged by Oxford Rail's recently released 57ft bogie Carflat wagon, based on those constructed from ex-LMS carriage underframes, now available in BR bauxite (Cat No. OR76CAR001/002) and BR 'Motorail' blue (OR76CAR003) liveries while Bachmann's BR Mk 1 derivative of the 23ton 63ft 6in bogie Carflat in BR bauxite (38-900) and BR blue (38-901/38-902) is currently under development. Also suitable in 'OO' are the Bachmann/Invicta Model Rail BR Mk 1 CCT in BR maroon (39-550Z) and BR blue (39-551Z), while Bachmann's BR Mk 1 57ft 'Motorail' GUV is offered in BR blue/grey (39-274A) and BR InterCity liveries (39-276), plus the manufacturer's plain BR blue (39-272C) model could be renumbered accordingly. Kernow Model Rail Centre also commissioned a limited run of Bachmann's BR Mk 1 57ft GUV in BR (SR) green as S86804 with accompanying 'Surbiton Okehampton Car Carrier' roofboards (39-273Z), representing the prototype which operated for a time in the early 1960s.

Hornby's London and North Eastern Railway (LNER) extra-long CCT (R6833D) and London, Midland & Scottish Railway (LMS) CCT (R6641) in BR crimson represent vehicles which remained in service for many years, while its range also contains an articulated two-tier car-carrying

VEHICLE DESIGNATIONS	
BG	Gangwayed Brake
BCK	Corridor Brake Composite
BFK	Corridor Brake First
BSK	Corridor Brake Second
CK	Corridor Composite
FK	Corridor First
FO	Open First
GUV	General Utility Van ('Motorail')
RB	Restaurant Buffet
RBR	Restaurant Buffet Refurbished
RFO	Restaurant First Open
RMB	Restaurant Miniature Buffet
RU	Restaurant Unclassed
SK	Corridor Second
SLE	Sleeper Either Class
SLEP	Sleeper Either Class with Pantry
SLF	Sleeper First
SLS	Sleeper Standard
SLSTP	Sleeper Standard Twin Berth with Pantry
SO	Open Second
TSO	Tourist Open Second

wagon in BR 'Motorail' livery (R6397), based loosely on BR's CARTIC-4 vehicles. For those wishing to model a more accurate CARTIC-4 model in 'OO', an etched kit was introduced some years ago through Intercity Models.

For modellers of East Coast Main Line and some cross-country workings to the South West, a 'OO' gauge kit of the BR Mk 1 Newton Chambers TCV is available from Southern Pride Models for the BR maroon (EMW1a) or BR blue/grey (EMW1b) period.

Ready-to-run passenger accommodation is well-represented through Bachmann, Hornby and Replica Railways' portfolio of pre-nationalisation and BR Mk 1, Mk 2 and Mk 3 seated and sleeper vehicles, although the small fleet of BR Mk 1 Corridor Brake First (BFK) vehicles utilised on 'Motorail' services is not currently available ready-to-run in 'OO'. We have replaced this carriage type with a BR Mk 1 BCK or BR Mk 2 BFK where necessary in the formations.

For a finishing touch, Sankey Scenics has recently introduced a range of high-resolution BR 'Motorail' detailing packs, suitable for the BR blue period in 'OO'. Each pack contains »

USEFUL LINKS	
Bachmann	www.bachmann.co.uk
Heljan	www.heljan.dk
Hornby	www.hornby.com
Invicta Model Rail	www.invictamodelrail.com
Kernow Model Rail Centre	www.kernowmodelrailcentre.com
Oxford Rail	www.oxfordrail.com
Replica Railways	www.replicarailways.co.uk
Sankey Scenics	www.sankeyscenics.co.uk
Southern Pride Models	www.southernpridemodels.co.uk

Left: **Class 50 50048** *Dauntless* skirts the estuary at Teignmouth with a lengthy 'Motorail' service from Kensington Olympia to St Austell on August 5 1979. *John Chalcraft/ Railphotoprints.co.uk.*

EXAMPLE "MOTORAIL" FORMATIONS

Bulleid rebuilt 'Merchant Navy' 4-6-2 BR lined green, late crests (Hornby), BR Mk 1 GUV, GUV, GUV, GUV,GUV, Bulleid semi-open BSK, BR Mk 1 RB, SO – BR green
Date: 1960 **Service:** Surbiton to Okehampton **Location:** Surbiton

Gresley 'A4' 4-6-2 BR lined green, late crests (Bachmann/Hornby), BR Mk 1 BSO, FK, RB, FO, GUV, GUV, GUV, GUV, GUV – BR maroon
Date: 1962 **Service:** Anglo Scottish Car Carrier **Location:** Grantham

Class 47 BR two-tone green with small yellow warning panel (Bachmann/Heljan/ViTrains), BR Mk 1 FK, FK, RB, FK, BCK, Carflat*, Carflat*, Carflat*, Carflat*, Carflat*, LMS Stove R - BR maroon except *BR bauxite
Date: 1966 **Service:** Newton-le-Willows to Stirling **Location:** Stirling

Class 42 BR blue with full yellow ends (Bachmann), BR Mk 1 BCK, SLSTP, SLSTP, FK, FK, FK, 'Motorail' Carflat*, Carflat*, Carflat* - BR blue/grey except *BR blue
Date: 1971 **Service:** Newton Abbot to Sutton Coldfield **Location:** Tiverton Junction

Class 33 BR blue (Heljan), BR Mk 1 BSO, FK, SLSTP, SLSTP, 'Motorail' Carflat*, Carflat*, Carflat*, Carflat* - BR blue/grey except *BR blue
Date: 1975 **Service:** Brockenhurst to Stirling **Location:** Totton

Class 52 BR blue (Dapol/Heljan), BR Mk 1 BSK, FK, RU, FO, FK, 'Motorail' Carflat*, Carflat*, Carflat*, Carflat* - BR blue/grey except *BR blue
Date: 1975 **Service:** St Austell to Kensington Olympia **Location:** Exeter St Davids

Class 50 BR blue (Hornby), BR Mk 1 FK, FK, RU, FK, BR Mk 2 BFK, 'Motorail' Carflat*, Carflat*, Carflat*, Carflat* - BR blue/grey except *BR blue
Date: 1976 **Service:** Kensington Olympia to St Austell **Location:** Dawlish

Class 47 BR blue (Bachmann/Heljan/ViTrains), BR Mk 3 SLE, SLEP, SLE, SLEP, SLE, BR Mk 1 BG, GUV*, GUV*, GUV* - BR blue/grey except *BR blue
Date: 1983 **Service:** Kings Cross to Edinburgh **Location:** Dunbar

Class 85 BR blue (Bachmann), four BR Mk 1 FKs, BR Mk 2 BCK, 'Motorail' Carflat*, Carflat*, Carflat*, Carflat* - BR InterCity except *BR blue
Date: 1987 **Service:** Euston to Stirling **Location:** Preston

Class 37/4 BR InterCity Mainline (Bachmann/ViTrains), BR Mk 1 GUV, GUV, GUV, BR Mk 3 SLE, SLEP, SLE, BR Mk 2d BSO – BR InterCity
Date: 1992 **Service:** Fort William to London Euston **Location:** Fort William

accurately dimensioned 'Motorail' Carflat side panels and carriage destination boards with sixteen different route-specific options available including London to Perth, Newton Abbot to Kensington, Inverness to York, Kensington to Penzance, Birmingham to Stirling and more. Both standard blue-backed BR Mk 1 carriage roof destination boards and BR Western Region style destination side panels feature in the range, as does a pack to detail a 'Motorail' terminal too, with signage, platform letters and numbers, posters, direction signs, speed limits, train departure boards and more. The route specific packs also include a sheet of blue 'Motorail' windscreen protectors, while bespoke packs with your own destinations are also offered.

Given the varied forms of car-carrying services, most ran to quite lengthy formations with some freight services formed in excess of 20 bogie Carflat wagons, while some passenger formations were also incredibly long (and heavy) by the time seated and sleeper vehicles had been added. On the other hand, there were a few services which ran with as few as two seated vehicles, two sleeper vehicles and four bogie Carflats – easily modellable.

The following selection of prototype formations represents a small snap-shot of the many services operated and enable realistic, ready-to-run car-carrying trains to be modelled in 'OO'. Whilst not exhaustive, plausible train formations can be developed with a little modeller's licence and selective compression, due to the sheer length that some formations ran to. Some currently unavailable ready-to-run vehicles (BR Mk 1 TCV/BFK) have been substituted with alternatives, where necessary, while formations have been limited to a maximum of nine vehicles, although they can be lengthened or reduced further to suit individual needs. ∎

FORT WILLIAM 'MOTORAIL' TERMINAL

On a damp day at Fort William in 1992 a Class 08 collects the single 'Motorail' GUV from the rear of the arriving sleeper to shunt it to the unloading dock. Mark Chivers.

The unloading dock is a simple concrete ramp which leads up to the GUV van. Mark Chivers.

Representing a 1970s 'Motorail' service, a Hornby Class 50 heads a rake of blue and grey stock lead by a trio of Oxford Rail 57ft Carflats loaded with Oxford Diecast vehicles.

Unloading the GUVs is as simple as starting the cars and driving them down the ramp. Mark Chivers.

Rail freight *rethink*

Three decades ago, British Rail's goods operations underwent perhaps the biggest shake-up in its history with the creation of five new freight sectors, a move that ushered in a colourful new era which eventually led to privatisation, as **EVAN GREEN-HUGHES** explains.

IN THE LATTER HALF OF THE 1980s, our railways were coming under increasing scrutiny from those in power. Margaret Thatcher had been returned for a third term as Prime Minister in 1987 and her Conservative government had established its policy of a strong economy based on low inflation, cost cutting and privatisation. However, although starved of investment and with some of their periphery activities such as hotels and ships sold off, the railways had so far remained in state hands, with those in power unable to agree on the best way forward.

Productivity was a major issue for the government, and with it the vast cost of supporting the loss-making railway. British Rail had only been able to deliver savings of 5% in the 10 years up to 1980, despite route and service closures. An independent report at that time had recommended splitting up the railway system into sectors to better concentrate management effort and that had resulted in the formation of InterCity, Provincial Services, SouthEast, Parcels and Freight as separate entities. From then on, and in a complete break with the past, all investment proposals had to be offered up for approval with each being carefully scrutinised as to whether they were value for money or not.

The first attempt to change the way the freight sector worked had been in 1977 when Speedlink was formed in an attempt to stem the loss of wagonload traffic to road transport. Dedicated management worked on the introduction of a high-speed inter-urban service which used air braked long-wheelbase wagons, with reduced shunting times providing attractive delivery times. At first this proved very successful with the 29 trains operated per day initially rising to 150 within seven years. Working alongside this was the Freightliner container operation which was also proving to be a great success in retaining goods on the railway.

In 1982 the rest of the traffic was vested in a new division which was called Railfreight, which took over everything not operated by Speedlink or Freightliner, integrating all forms of traffic with each other and at the same time splitting them from either regional control or any association with passenger activities.

Locomotives allocated to this sector were soon »

Railfreight Distribution Class 86s 86631 and 86604 wait at Carlisle with tanks from Larbert and the Mossend-Willesden ABS as DVT 82110 leaves with a Glasgow - Euston working (propelled by 87028) on July 13 1991. John Chalcraft/Railphotoprints.co.uk.

Below: Re-engined Class 37/9 37906, one of two fitted with a Ruston engine, makes a smoky exit from Wednesbury with steel empties returning to Cardiff Tidal sidings on September 6 1989. The locomotive is finished in Railfreight Metals sector livery.
Brian Robbins/Railphotoprints.co.uk.

Coal was a major revenue source for Railfreight and all 50 of the Class 58s were allocated to this sector. On January 22 1994 58004 draws a rake of HAAs through Bentinck Colliery loading silo before departure to Ratcliffe Power Station. Steve Turner/Railphotoprints.co.uk.

identified with the application of a new livery, a rather uninspiring allover grey, but with cabs or nose ends painted in warning panel yellow and with bodysides adorned with a very large BR double arrow symbol. These colours first appeared on the new Class 58s in 1982 and were then gradually rolled out to other engines assigned to the division. Later this scheme was enhanced by the addition of a red stripe along the solebar or bottom of the body.

Behind the scenes

While the colour change to the locomotives and rolling stock were noticeable to the casual observer, what wasn't so obvious were the changes that were going on behind the scenes. Assets such as rolling stock and buildings that had previously been shared between various railway operations were reorganised so that they could be dedicated to one form of traffic and therefore used more intensively than before: crews were allocated only to freight trains with rosters organised so that each man did more work and management was streamlined with elements of waste cut out.

Despite this reorganisation, many customers complained that too much of the old BR attitude remained, and that there was an inflexible attitude to changes in traffic flows or business conditions.

Foster Yeoman had a substantial flow of quarried materials from the Mendips to London but had experienced considerable difficulties with the reliability of BR's Class 56s when used on its traffic. As a result it purchased four US-built Class 59s, these later being joined by four more for Amey Roadstone and six for National Power. These were all operated by BR, which also provided the crews – but the locomotives were owned and maintained privately.

After only five years of Railfreight, there was then another change when it was felt that more efficiencies could be made by further dividing freight activities so that differing types of flow would come under their own individual management, and in turn be better able react to market requirements. An advantage of this was that those in power also wished to know exactly which parts of the freight operation were actually profitable, as there was already a long-term eye being kept on prospects for rail privatisation, even »

Class 47 47219 *Arnold Kunzler* passes Fenny Compton with 4M60 1.10pm Southampton MCT-Birmingham Lawley Street Freightliner service on June 20 1992. John Chalcraft/Railphotoprints.co.uk.

Below: Construction sector Romanian Class 56 56033 passes the site of Box station at the head of 4C13 - the 11.11am Calvert-Bath/Bristol waste train empties - on April 30 1993. John Chalcraft/Railphotoprints.co.uk.

Railfreight's traffic types included stock movements as well as the more valuable bulk goods flows. Class 47/0 47210 *Blue Circle Cement* runs up the relief lines of the Great Western Main Line near Lower Basildon with the 12.17pm Didcot-West Ruislip London Transport stock transfer working on April 11 1992. John Chalcraft/Railphotoprints.co.uk.

though it was then still not official Conservative party policy.

As a result, two organisations were created, each of which had a number of sub-sectors. By far the smallest was Railfreight Distribution which was to handle intermodal work and wagonload freight. Much larger was Trainload Freight which was to deal with unit trains, that contained only one type of cargo. This organisation had a number of sub-sectors, these dealing with coal, construction materials, metals and petroleum products. A new livery was planned for all freight locomotives, which was to be a two colour grey scheme, which was far more attractive than the former Railfreight version.

So that each sector could better identify its assets, each locomotive would have a full height decal on each side which was to represent the traffic worked by each sector. Railfreight Distribution's decal consisted of two red diamonds on a yellow background interlocked with a red square while Railfreight General, which quickly became part of Distribution, used alternate red and yellow rectangles instead of the diamonds. For the block traffic, Trainload Freight used four different locomotive decals - engines used on coal traffic received a large yellow square with four black diamonds in it and offset onto a black square, those employed on construction and aggregates traffic had alternate blue and yellow squares offset by a larger blue square, locomotives working metals trains had alternate blue and yellow chevrons instead of squares while those used on petroleum traffic had the blue and yellow parts of their decals represented as waves.

Block profits

As had been identified by the Beeching Report more than 20 years earlier, by far the most profitable type of traffic for rail was that which ran in block trains with the whole train travelling from the point of loading to the point of delivery and it was this traffic that was vested in Trainload Freight. In fact at this time around 80% of British

Rail's freight income came from this type of traffic with movement of block trains being the only consistently profitable part of BR's freight operation.

It had long been recognised that profitability increased with train length and for this reason British Rail had decided that its new Trainload Freight sector should be equipped with a new fleet of suitable high-powered locomotives. These engines, later known as the Class 60s, were built by Brush at Loughborough at a cost of £120million, a sum that could now be justified under government guidelines due to the profitability of the traffic which the new engines would now work. The Class 60s were a major technological advance on any previous British-made product and had huge haulage power, enabling single machines to replace pairs of older locomotives, such as Class 33s and 31s, with subsequent improvements in operating efficiency. Unfortunately, although the locomotives were strong they proved not to be very reliable and there were to be many modifications and upgrades before they were all to be got to work in a satisfactory manner.

Also continuing during this period was the upgrading of rolling stock used on block trains. For many years British Rail had relied on the use of four-wheel wagons for all freight traffic but during the 1960s and 1970s there had been a steady move towards high-capacity bogie wagons. For improved efficiency on its aggregates traffic, Foster Yeoman had obtained some bogie box wagons that had once worked on the Teeside ore traffic and had since added others to the fleet, although these had been new boxes built on second-hand running gear. At the same time new high-capacity bogie tank wagons were being used on oil and petroleum trains and both proved that it was more efficient to use bigger vehicles, partly because they could be worked at higher speed but also because less of the train's length was taken up with the space between the wagons. Such efficiencies enabled Trainload Freight to make an economic case for further investment.

> *"The Class 60s were a major technological advance."*
>
> **EVAN GREEN-HUGHES**

Trainload Freight proved to be everything that those who had formed it had hoped and within four years of its formation it was returning 8% on its capital assets, a figure that exceeded even that asked for by the government. By this time it was doing around £500m worth of business each year and was able to make a profit of around 14%. However there were some flows that were not so profitable, with cement being one form of traffic that was operating on a very slender margin, and as the sector was now run on purely commercial lines a pricing policy was adopted which was designed to prune out the less profitable flows and retain the rest. About three million tons of business a year was lost in this exercise but the company was able as a result to shed about half its locomotive fleet and 40% of its wagons and report, although briefly, even more profit.

Wagon load diminishes

While block trains were proving to be a money spinner, the same was not true for those operated by Railfreight Distribution, which now included trains formerly worked by

The fleet of 100 Class 60s represented a £120million investment by British Rail for its Railfreight sectors. Construction marked Class 60 60081 *Bleaklow Hill* is held at signals outside Cardiff Canton as it heads a Port Talbot-Llanwern Iron Ore service on June 23 1993. Brian Robbins/Railphotoprints.co.uk.

Speedlink and Freightliner. This division found it very difficult to compete with road transport, particularly where each consignment consisted of only one or two wagons at a time.

The situation was not helped by a continuing review of goods yards which found that there were many used by a small number of trains each week and which did not come anywhere near to covering their running costs. As a result many were closed with the intention that goods would be taken by road to the next most convenient yard. This had the inevitable result that manufacturers discovered that it was far simpler and cost effective to leave the goods on the road for their entire journey. The only wagonload traffic that proved to be viable was that travelling over long distances and, in many cases, this was retained by combining flows from more than one source to make up a full-length train.

There was some success for other traffic allocated to this sector. Materials such as sand and timber which did not generate sufficient volume to be included in the Construction sector of Trainload Freight provided a good volume of »

Above: **The early introduction of the Railfreight sector liveries took time to take effect with previous liveries remaining in service alongside the new. Petroleum sector Class 37 37294 leads 'Redstripe' 37/3 37374 through Sonning Cutting with a Robeston-Langley oil working on April 7 1990.**
John Chalcraft/Railphotoprints.co.uk.

Left: **Within a few years of the sectors being created locomotives were found at the head of trains which didn't match their decals. In April 1991 Petroleum liveried Class 56 56036 approaches Earlswood, on the Brighton main line south of Redhill, with a train of RMC aggregate hoppers for Crawley.** Brian Stephenson.

Below: **Railfreight Distribution was responsible for handling traffic to and from the Channel Tunnel following its opening, with many trains hauled by an ageing fleet of Class 47s. On May 18 1998 RFD Class 47s 47365 *Diamond Jubilee* and 47219 *Arnold Kunzler* pass Charing with an up car train from Dollands Moor and the Channel Tunnel.** Brian Stephenson.

business, as did the transport of grain and china clay while the sector was also kept afloat by the growing traffic in the transport of new cars and commercial vehicles, many of which were beginning to be imported in large numbers. Also allocated to this sector was Channel Tunnel traffic, which was a little odd as at that time the tunnel was not open for freight and in the event when it was this traffic was taken away and dealt with separately. Particularly pleasing was the growth of container traffic, building on the pioneering work that had been done in the 1960s.

It is worth mentioning at this point that there was another even smaller sector formed during the 1988 reorganisation and that was Railfreight General. This was intended as a 'catch all' for any traffic that didn't fit within the Trainload Freight or the Railfreight Distribution remit and at its inception it was allocated a fleet of only four locomotives. Such a small organisation was obviously going to be ineffective and within two years it was disbanded and also amalgamated into the Railfreight Distribution part of the business.

> *"Railfreight could have served the railways well for years."*
> **EVAN GREEN-HUGHES**

New horizons

Had privatisation not been on the horizon it is likely that the 1988 reorganisation of Railfreight would have been a model that could have served the railways well for many years. Certainly, trainload traffic was performing very well as were some aspects of the more general traffic. However to achieve adequate financial performance it had been found necessary to abandon some flows and to close down some yards and terminals, perhaps to the detriment of the country as a whole.

Investment was also inadequate during this period with the Class 60s proving to be the only new locomotives provided for freight operations during the whole six-year period that the sectorised system was in operation, resulting in too many trains being worked by outdated and inefficient motive power.

The next reorganisation for freight traffic was triggered by two political events. In 1991 the European Union issued its First Railway Directive which set out a framework for all railways to allow open access operations on their infrastructure. This directive also required member states to ensure that entities operating infrastructure and the trains themselves were separated and also run on a commercial basis. Effectively this meant that the state could not operate both the trains and the infrastructure and it is this piece of legislation, still in force today, that is conveniently forgotten by those who propose the re-nationalisation of our railway system.

Two years later the UK Railways Act set out how this was to be achieved in this country. It abolished British Rail's statutory monopoly of freight services and proposed that goods operations be prepared for transfer to private ownership by splitting them into divisions. Rather surprisingly these divisions were not to be on the lines of those sectors which already existed but were to be organised on geographical lines, but with Channel Tunnel, mail and container traffic excluded for separate privatisation.

In 1994 three shadow companies were formed, still in state ownership but run in a businesslike manner and in a way that would facilitate their sale to the private sector. Although based on geographical lines, the companies were formed in such a way as they could provide some competition for each other. Transrail Freight had the largest operating area which included Scotland, Wales and the north; this company retained the former Trainload triple grey livery, replacing the decals with its own version of a large white T on a blue circular background surrounded by red and white circles and with two red lines underneath.

The second company, Mainline Freight, was allocated an area centred round South East England, East Anglia and the East Midlands and it introduced an aircraft blue livery which had a white line along its centre. Their logo, which was a number of circles on a white line and above the company name, was carried on the bodyside underneath the central white line. Finally came Loadhaul, which operated in the north east and which was allocated the bulk of the coal and steel traffic. Its locomotives were given black bodysides with orange sections towards each end and with a large grey, black and orange logo.

During this period Channel Tunnel traffic, which had been much less prominent than had been expected, and Freightliner's container trains continued to be operated by Railfreight Distribution which continued to use the former two-colour grey scheme.

Coat of colour

This was an exceptionally colourful time for freight operations as not only were there locomotives and trains operating in Railfreight Distribution, Loadhaul, Transrail and Mainline liveries but also there were many variations and one offs as new decals were applied to earlier liveries. Some older locomotives were also retained past their normal sell-by date due to problems with the Class 92s which had been ordered for Channel Tunnel work but which were causing signalling interference issues, leading to

them being banned from some routes.

However, these arrangements were not to last for long as by this time the government was looking for buyers for these companies and this led to a sale being organised by competitive tender. Despite the government's best efforts none of the prospective buyers favoured the idea of buying a third of the country's freight business, instead preferring the alternative of bringing it all back under one roof once again. The winning bid came from a consortium headed by the American railroad Wisconsin Central which subsequently bought Loadhaul, Mainline and Transrail for £225m in February 1996 and with the three companies became the owners of more than 900 locomotives and 19,000 wagons. This consortium had already bid for, and obtained, Rail Express Systems, which ran parcels and mail trains and later added the loss-making Railfreight Distribution to its portfolio and became virtually a monopoly provider of freight services to the country, exactly the opposite of what had been planned.

Within a year the freight sector had been reorganised once again, with everything brought

under common management under the branding of English, Welsh & Scottish Railways. Soon efficiencies had been introduced which enabled the company to reduce its rates to customers by 30% and in May 1996, with the freight sector's new owners said to be appalled at the state of existing British-built traction, 280 brand new Class 66 and 67 locomotives were ordered.

So ended one of the most colourful and turbulent times for rail-borne freight. There had been two major reorganisations in only eight years, a period that had seen numerous sectors and companies come and go and a monopoly broken up only to be reformed once again. Much business had been lost, and some had been won, old ways of moving goods had been discontinued and some traffic that perhaps should have remained on the rails was no longer with us.

Those looking to model the diesel and electric era but who want to see colourful and varied freight trains in different liveries might well want to consider the Railfreight period as a good basis for a layout for it was definitely one of the most interesting of the last 50 years. ∎

Digital sound
DECODERS

EQUIPMENT GUIDE

As sound gains popularity, the number of suitable decoders has multiplied.
MARK CHIVERS examines some of the most popular options.

The range of readily available digital sound decoders continues to grow offering more choice. Here a Heljan *Falcon*, fitted with a LokSound V4.0 8-pin decoder with a Howes Models sound file, prepares to depart Grosvenor Square – *Hornby Magazine's* Yearbook project layout from 2016.
Mike Wild/*Hornby Magazine.*

DIGITAL COMMAND CONTROL (DCC) sound has transformed the hobby for many, adding a level of realism that enables model locomotives to better represent their prototype counterparts.

Initially, the choice of suitable decoders and their abilities was limited, but today we are graced with an incredible selection of decoders offering the ability to control sound, lighting effects and additional functionality such as smoke generators in steam locomotives.

At the same time, the quality of sound projects has improved as the technology and thirst for this area has developed to enable larger sound files to be accommodated with finer adjustments to suit individual needs, better sound quality and more functionality. Today, most digital sound decoders enable up to 28 individual sound functions to be accessed on a suitable DCC command station, offering an impressive array of audio options such as numerous whistles or warning horns, wheel flange squeal, brakes and even cab doors closing and track detonator sounds. In addition, the ability to operate the growing number of lighting options has seen functionality improve within the decoder

types allowing directional lighting, individually controlled head and tail lights, interior lighting and even steam locomotive firebox flicker to be replicated in miniature.

Technology does come at a cost, however, and until recently a typical high quality DCC sound decoder would cost around £100, but this is changing as the market adapts to a growing selection of budget and mid-level sound decoders, now starting from less than £40. These new entrants are still offering a good quality product, but usually there are limits to some of their abilities.

With a top end digital sound decoder, you can fine-tune multiple onboard Configuration Values (CVs) to hone the performance of individual locomotives and, if you wish, have the sound project reprogrammed by a third-party digital specialist and a new project added. With budget digital sound decoders, they may feature a limited number of CVs with sound projects which can't be replaced, while some mid-level digital sound decoders also offer multiple sound sets for different locomotive classes, available at the change of a CV setting. The onboard audio on the budget and mid-level decoders is often very good and, when matched with a good quality

speaker, the results can be spectacular.

As these new decoder types become established, it is anticipated that more modellers will be encouraged to give DCC sound a try, and in turn upgrade to top end digital decoder types which can be 're-blown' with new sound files as upgrades to projects and improvements are introduced, or even a completely different locomotive sound project.

A large number of original UK sound projects are available direct from digital sound specialists (see Useful Links) and an increasing selection of model railway retailers. Some specialists also develop their own bespoke style of operation, offering added variety such as special braking techniques or coasting qualities to sound projects.

With such a growing market, in this equipment guide we focus on five popular DCC sound decoder types featuring UK sound projects and compare their abilities in terms of power handling, sound output, functionality and price. Whilst not exhaustive, it aims to offer an introduction to what is available and encourage you to explore further the wealth of digital sound decoders. ∎

Hornby Twin Track Sound

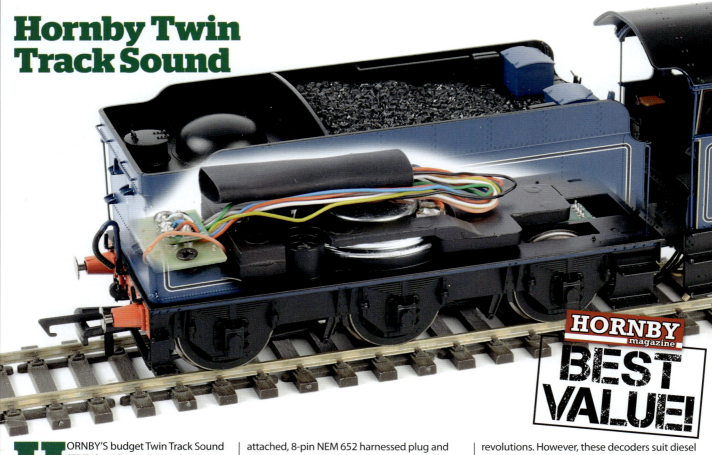

BEST VALUE!

HORNBY'S budget Twin Track Sound (TTS) digital sound decoders have been available in factory-fitted form, but during September 2017, the company released the first of its solo-packaged 8-pin decoders with a £39.99 price tag.

Initial solo-packaged releases planned include Class 31 (Cat No. R8101), Class 37 (R8102), Class 47 (R8103), Class 60 (R8104) and Class 67 (R8105) diesels and Gresley 'A1'/'A3' 4-6-2 (R8106), Gresley 'A4' 4-6-2 (R8107), Peppercorn 'A1' 4-6-2 (R8108), Collett 'King' 4-6-0 (R8109) and Collett 'Castle' 4-6-0 (R8110) steam locomotives.

Each of the TTS decoders measures 25mm x 14mm x 5mm and comes with a 28mm diameter round or 40mm x 20mm 8ohm speaker

attached, 8-pin NEM 652 harnessed plug and an informative instruction manual outlining supported CVs with hints and tips on operation and customisable volume adjustments.

Rated at 1amp peak power, 0.5amp continuous motor load, it is suitable for use with most modern models. Up to 19 function keys are supported on TTS steam decoders (F0-F18) while up to 26 function keys (F0-F25) are supported on TTS diesel examples and include a selection of whistle and horn sounds, wheel slip, guard's whistle and even a fireman's breakfast on steam examples – a novel if perhaps frivolous inclusion.

In terms of the onboard sound files, the diesel classes include sounds specific to individual locomotive types, while some of the steam classes appear to comprise some sound files shared between decoders, and there is a lack of synchronisation between the exhaust beat and the wheel

revolutions. However, these decoders suit diesel sounds very well and offer much better output in line with the locomotive performance as well as manual power notching to allow light and heavy loads to be more easily represented.

Amongst their limitations, Hornby's TTS decoders cannot be reprogrammed by third-party specialists, features just two sound channels – effectively the main engine sounds and one function key operated sound at a time. Whilst this may sound limiting, for most it is effective and adequate.

CV support is limited, but this three-function decoder can be used with 14, 28 and 128 speed steps, supports short and long addresses, offers directional lighting, and includes an auxiliary function too. Whilst acceleration (CV3) and deceleration (CV4) levels are accessible for determining speed settings, start voltage (CV2), mid voltage (CV6) and top voltage (CV5) settings cannot be modified, but it does include adjustable Back EMF load compensation (CV10).

On test, we found that reducing the Back EMF value on our Class 31 TTS decoder, fitted to Hornby's high-fidelity model, improved its low speed performance. It should also be noted that while Hornby's TTS decoders will operate on conventional analogue controlled layouts, the onboard sounds will not play. There have also been some compatbility issues with specific operating system, including Dynamis, which Hornby is currently looking into.

Hornby's TTS decoder is a great introduction to digital sound with a good selection of onboard sounds, responsive control and driveability, all at a keen price, too.

D 5551

ESU LokSound V4.0

ELECTRONIC Solutions Ulm (ESU) introduced its LokSound decoder in 1999 and since then has been a leading exponent of digital sound, which includes its ESU LokSound V4.0 decoders.

The current family of LokSound V4.0 digital sound decoders offers an array of connection options including 6-pin NEM651 (Cat No. 56499), 8-pin NEM652 (54400) and PluX12 (55440) harness style connectors along with wireless 21MTC interface (54499) and PluX22 (56498) direct plug styles. In addition, the LokSound micro V4.0 range includes 6-pin NEM 651 (54800), 8-pin NEM652 (56899), PluX12 (55800) and Next18 (54898) variants for limited space 'OO', 'N', and 'TT' applications, while for larger scale modellers, the LokSound V4.0 XL comes in two formats with screw terminals (54500) and pin connectors (54599).

Offered blank or with a wide selection of UK sound projects from dedicated suppliers, ESU's LokSound V4.0 decoders are fully reprogrammable with new sound projects, when required, which can be 're-blown' to the decoder by third-party suppliers. Many factory-fitted ready-to-run DCC sound models feature ESU's family of decoders, with Bachmann and Hornby having opted for LokSound V3.0, V3.5 and V4.0 examples in their products in the past.

The standard version has an impressive specification which supports a 1.1amp maximum continuous motor load, has four 0.25amp function outputs, also includes two logic outputs – effectively six function outputs in total and comes with a SUSI (Serial User Standard Interface) interface to allow additional circuits to be connected too. Measuring 30.3mm x 15.5mm x 5.5mm, the decoder comes with a 23mm diameter or 40mm x 20mm 4ohm speaker and

sound chamber. Up to eight digital sounds can be played simultaneously, thanks to its onboard polyphonic sound channels and it can store 276 seconds of audio within its 32Megabit memory.

Two and four-digit address programming, 14, 28 and 128 speed steps are supported while comprehensive interrogation of CVs is possible, including fine-tuning steam locomotive 'chuff-rates', lighting styles and effects, brightness adjustment and more. Programming can be undertaken on the main line (PoM) or on a dedicated programming track and brake modes from Lenz, Selectrix, Roco and Marklin, full function mapping capability, RailComPlus detection and 29 function keys (F0-F28) are also supported.

Analogue control is also supported, and engine running sounds will operate as more power is applied to the tracks in conventional DC mode.

Operating characteristics can be further improved with the addition of optional power packs, offering up to two seconds' uninterrupted

movement if the track power is interrupted. Firmware can also be updated through ESU's LokProgrammer device (53451) and a computer.

ESU's LokSound V4.0 micro decoder supports a 0.75amp continuous motor power and comes with four 0.15amp function outputs, two logic outputs and is supplied with a 16mm x 25mm speaker and sound chamber. At just 25mm x 10.6mm x 3.8mm it is one of the smallest sound decoders available.

ESU's LokSound V4.0 family of digital sound decoders offers outstanding programming capability, extensive fine-tuning ability and phenomenal smooth control and is well supported with third-party UK sound options Prices are £95-£120 for standard 'OO' and 'N' scale projects and £175-£190 for large scale decoders.

ESU LokSound Select

ESU'S LokSound Select family of digital sound decoders is primarily intended for the US market, although a small number of UK ready-to-run factory-fitted digital sound models have been equipped with this decoder type, including examples from Bachmann, and most recently, Realtrack Models for its 'OO' gauge Class 156 Diesel Multiple Unit.

Available in 8-pin NEM652 harness (Cat No. 73400) and wireless 21MTC interface (73900) formats, these 1.1amp continuous motor current rated decoders are well-specified and similar in many respects to their V4.0 cousins and come with six function outputs, 32Megabit memory capacity, Back EMF, function mapping, lighting effects, adjustable brightness and adjustable CV programming. Measuring just 30mm x 15mm, the audio amplifier output is 2watts at 4ohms, with eight sound channels enabling up to eight sounds to be operated simultaneously, while individual volume slots can be adjusted, as well as the overall master control volume. The LokSound Select is usually supplied with a 23mm diameter speaker.

With up to 276 seconds of audio storage available, it can produce more than 20 individual

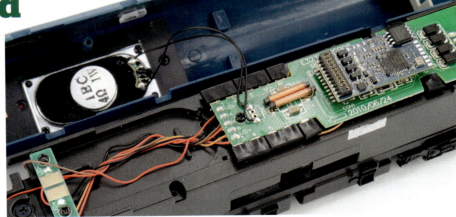

sounds, offers excellent functionality, and supports 29 function keys (F0-F28). Again, optional capacitors and power packs can be added to provide up to two seconds of uninterrupted movement without track power, and the decoder firmware is also updateable.

For limited space installations, a LokSound Select Micro (73800) digital sound decoder is also available with 8-pin NEM652 harness, measuring 25mm x 10.6mm x 3.8mm with a 0.75amp continuous motor current rating and four function outputs.

As they were originally designed to compete with keener priced US sound options in mind,

the LokSound Select decoders are limited in their ability to be 're-blown' with alternative sound projects and it is not possible to rework them with third-party UK sound projects. They can, however, be 're-blown' by the originators of the sound project or through ESU's library of LokSound Select sound projects – although these are mainly of overseas prototypes.

Whilst originally offering a cheaper alternative to the LokSound V4.0, exchange rates have increased the retail price for single decoders in the UK, but it can still prove cost-effective for factory-fitted ready-to-run models containing LokSound Select technology.

Soundtraxx Econami UK

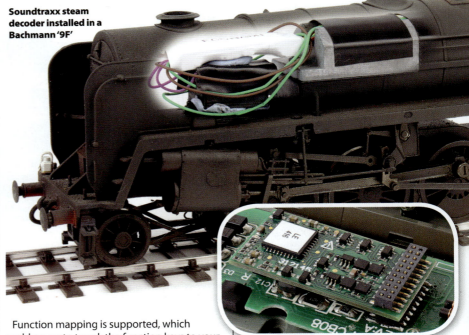

Soundtraxx steam decoder installed in a Bachmann '9F'

AMERICAN manufacturer Soundtraxx recently introduced its Econami digital sound decoders pre-loaded with UK steam and diesel sounds.

UK steam versions are available in three formats as a 1amp four function decoder with wire harness (Cat No. 88101), 2amp six function decoder with wire harness (Cat No. 881102) and 1amp six function 21-pin wireless decoder (881106), and similarly for UK diesel versions (882101/882102/882106) respectively.

What differentiates these decoders from their competitors is the inclusion of multiple sound projects on the same decoder. Steam examples come with five fully functional projects including GWR 'Prairie' 2-6-2T, LMS Stanier '8F' 2-8-0, BR '4MT' 4-6-0, BR '5MT' 4-6-0 and LNER 'A4' 4-6-2 sounds, while the diesel examples include six choices with BR classes 20, 31, 37, 47, 66 and Derby 'Lightweight' Diesel Multiple Unit audio. In addition, a raft of additional sounds can be selected through CV changes with multiple whistles from other motive power including a single London and North Eastern Railway chime and Southern Railway 'West Country' 4-6-2 options, while alternative diesel warning horns can be chosen too. The steam locomotive exhaust beat can be set to match wheel revolutions, with two or three-cylinder exhaust beats, selectable carriage door slams, cylinder drain cocks, coupling rod clanks and much more readily available through CVs.

Function mapping is supported, which enables you to tweak the function keys to your personal taste, with full explanation available in the downloadable instruction manual. Dynamic braking is possible through a function key by this method, and full details can be found in the manual.

Sound quality is good, thanks in part to the 2W 8ohm audio amplifier output with seven band equaliser and 16-bit sound, aiding 40 individual sounds and 20 lighting effects – accessible through the supported 29 function keys (F0-F28) – although not all are used. A suitable speaker is required to complete the sound installation.

Each decoder also contains onboard circuitry to manage its power requirements, which means that 'stay-alive' style capacitors can be added to improve performance if track power is briefly interrupted.

At £79.95 for 21-pin examples and £89.95 for the wire-only harness examples, they represent good value for money, particularly considering the multiple sound file options.

DCC SOUND DECODER COMPARISON									
Decoder:	**Hornby TTS**	**73900 LS Select**	**54400 LS V4.0**	**54499 LS V4.0**	**882106 UK Diesel**	**881106 UK Steam**	**881102 UK Steam**	**ZIMO MX644D**	**ZIMO MX645R**
Continuous motor current (max):	0.5amp	1.1amp	1.6amp	1.6amp	-	-	-	1.2amp	1.2amp
Motor stall current:	1amp	-	-	-	1amp	1amp	2amp	2.5amp	2.5amp
Function current (per output):	0.1amp	0.25amp	0.25amp	0.25amp	0.1amp	0.1amp	0.1amp	0.8amp (total)	0.8amp (total)
Dimensions (mm):	25 x 14 x 5	30 x 15.5 x 5.5	30.3 x 15.5 x 5.5	30.3 x 15.5 x 5.5	30.5 x 15.5 x 6.5	30.5 x 15.5 x 6.5	35 x 18 x 6	30 x 15 x 4	30 x 15 x 4
Function outputs:	3	6	4+2 logic	6 (4+2 logic)	6	6	6	8 (6+2 logic)	10 (8+2 logic)
Function output support:	F0-F25	F0-F28	F0-F28	F0-F28	F0-F28	F0-F28	F0-F28	F0-F28	F0-F28
Logic outputs:	x	-	✓	✓	x	x	x	✓	✓
Function mapping:	x	✓	✓	✓	✓	✓	✓	✓	✓
Audio amplifier output:	1.6W@8ohm	2W@4ohm	1.8W@4ohm	1.8W@4ohm	2W@8ohm	2W@8ohm	2W@8ohm	3W@4-8ohm	3W@4-8ohm
No. of sound channels:	2	8	8	8	12	12	12	8	8
Memory capacity:	-	32MBit	32MBit	32MBit	-	-	-	32MBit	32MBit
Connection:	Harness	Direct plug	Harness	Direct plug	Direct plug	Direct plug	Harness	Direct plug	Harness
Pin interface:	8-pin	21-pin	8-pin	21-pin	21-pin	21-pin	None	21-pin	8-pin
Railcom/Railcom Plus:	x	✓	✓	✓	x	x	x	✓	✓
Short addressing:	✓	✓	✓	✓	✓	✓	✓	✓	✓
Long addressing:	✓	✓	✓	✓	✓	✓	✓	✓	✓
Analogue DC operation:	✓ (6)	✓	✓	✓	✓	✓	✓	✓	✓
Directional lighting (F0):	✓	✓	✓	✓	✓	✓	✓	✓	✓
Lighting effects:	x	✓	✓	✓	✓	✓	✓	✓	✓
Reprogrammable:	x	x (3)	✓	✓	x	x	x	✓	✓
Pre-loaded UK sounds	✓	✓ (5)	(4)	(4)	✓	✓	✓	(4)	(4)
Speed steps:	14/28/128	14/28/128	14/28/128	14/28/128	14/28/128	14/28/128	14/28/128	14/28/128	14/28/128
Three-point and full speed curve:	(7)	✓	✓	✓	✓	✓	✓	✓	✓
SUSI interface:	x	x	✓	✓	x	x	x	✓	✓
Energy storage capability:	x	✓	✓	✓	✓	✓	✓	✓	✓
Service Mode programming:	✓	✓	✓	✓	✓	✓	✓	✓	✓
Operations Mode programming:	✓	✓	✓	✓	✓	✓	✓	✓	✓
Load compensation (Back EMF):	✓	✓	✓	✓	✓	✓	✓	✓	✓
Updateable firmware:	x	✓	✓	✓	-	-	-	✓	✓
Individual effects volume control:	✓	✓	✓	✓	✓	✓	✓	✓	✓
Speaker included:	✓	✓	✓	✓	x	x	x	x	x
Price:	£39.95	£110	from £95	from £95	£79.95	£79.95	£89.95	£92	£95

Notes: 1. Hard-wire. 2. No sound in analogue use. 3. Except originator of sound project. 4. Your choice of sound project can be added. 5. Factory-fitted DCC sound models (Bachmann/RealTrack etc). 6 Will operate on analogue controlled layouts, but without engine running sounds. 7. Limited configuration

Zimo sound decoders

AUSTRIAN manufacturer Zimo has been involved with digital control since the late 1970s and its extensive gamut of digital sound decoders includes its popular MX644 and MX645 family, which covers most connection options including 70mm wire-only harness (Cat No. MX645), 8-pin NEM652 harness (MX645R), 6-pin NEM651 harness (MX645F), PluX16 connector (MX645P16), PluX22 connector (MX645P22) and 21-pin MTC interface (MX644D).

Rated at 1.2amps continuous motor current, 2.5amp peak, they measure 30mm x 15mm x 4mm and include eight (MX644D) or ten (MX645) function outputs, with SUSI interface, logic level outputs and ability to operate two servos. 'Stay-alive' capability is possible utilising each decoder's onboard circuitry, while up to 276 seconds of audio can be stored within the 32 Megabit memory. Special lighting effects, Swiss mapping, brake on DC, Zimo brake control and Lenz asymmetric braking are fully supported, together with adjustable Back EMF, RailCom feedback and much more. It can also be programmed in service (programming track) and operations (PoM) mode, will operate on 14, 28 or 128 speed steps and works well with all motors including coreless examples, which are becoming increasingly prevalent in ready-to-run mechanisms.

Further examples within Zimo's range of digital sound decoders include a 0.8amp (1.5amp peak) Next18 version (MX658N18), which comprises four function outputs plus two logic level outputs, 3watt audio output on a 4ohm speaker, SUSI interface and measures 25mm x 10.5mm x 4mm. Smaller examples are also available including the 20mm x 11mm x 4mm 0.8amp (1.5amp peak) MX648 family of sub-miniature decoders including a wire-only harness example (MX648), 8-pin NEM652 (MX648R), 6-pin NEM651 (MX648F) and PluX16 interface (MX648P16). All bar the PluX16 example include six function outputs, two of which are through solder pads as logic level outputs. Up to two servos can be operated, while audio output is 1watt at 8ohms.

Zimo's 1amp MX649 miniature sound decoder range is ideal for limited space models, measuring 23mm x 9mm x 4mm, and features four function outputs, two solder pads for logic level outputs, servos, and SUSI. Six versions are available with a wire-only harness (MX649), 6-pin NEM651 mount on a circuit board with two additional speaker wires (MX649N), a similarly specified 90-degree mounted model (MX649L), 8-pin NEM652 harness (MX649R) and 6-pin NEM651 harness (MX649F).

For larger scale applications, ZIMO's MX695-MX699 family offer a choice of fully equipped and reduced functionality examples, 4amp-6amp continuous motor current, 10amp peak current, up to 15 function outputs, 32Megabit sound storage, smoke fan outputs, servo outputs, SUSI interface and 10watt audio output on 4-8ohm speakers.

To fully appreciate the level of finesse possible with Zimo technology, browse the downloadable manual or, if you have a compatible computer interface and software such as DecoderPro, copy the CV values across and explore the many options available to adjust and improve performance and characteristics. Alternatively, you could just plug the decoder in and enjoy its many facets. You will, though, need to acquire a suitable compatible speaker with Zimo producing a large family of 'cube' based speakers including some incredibly tiny options.

As you might imagine, a large selection of UK sound projects are available through Zimo retailers, which offer UK sound projects for steam, diesel, and electric prototypes with varying bespoke driving options, including coasting at the touch of a function key, multiple sound sets on one decoder and even braking through a function key. These are just a few examples offered by Zimo's digital sound specialists - see Useful Links for contact details. Each of the decoders mentioned can be re-blown with third-party sound projects, and firmware can be updated.

Offering some serious competition in the market place, Zimo decoders have become the decoder of choice for digital sound installations within *Hornby Magazine's* motive power exhibition fleet, due in part to their ease of use, intuitive control, impressive sound output and readily available driveable sound projects. With prices ranging from £90-£99 for MX644-MX658 series decoders and £140-£175 for large scale MX695-MX699 decoders, they also represent excellent value.

A factory fitted Zimo MX649 in a Graham Farish 'N' gauge 'Castle'.

HORNBY magazine OUR PICK

A Zimo MX644D installed in a 'OO' gauge Heljan 'O2' 2-8-0.

USEFUL LINKS	
Bachmann	www.bachmann.co.uk
Coastal DCC	www.coastaldcc.co.uk
DC Kits	www.dckits-devideos.co.uk
DCC Train Automation	www.dcctrainautomation.co.uk
Digitrains	www.digitrains.co.uk
ESU	www.esu.eu
Gaugemaster	www.gaugemaster.com
Hornby	www.hornby.com
Howes Models	www.howesmodels.co.uk
JMRI Decoderpro	www.jmri.org
Locoman Sounds	www.locomansounds.com
Mr Soundguy	www.mrsoundguy.co.uk
Olivia's Trains	www.oliviastrains.com
Realtrack Models	www.realtrackmodels.co.uk
Soundtraxx	www.soundtraxx.com
South West Digital	www.southwestdigital.co.uk
YouChoos	www.youchoos.co.uk
Wickness Models	www.wicknessmodels.co.uk
Zimo	www.zimo.at

Forward to 2018

The number of promised new locomotives may have fallen from 12 months ago, but more models have been released during 2017 than in many previous years. **MIKE WILD** looks ahead to 2018 and evaluates what our manufacturers have to offer in the future.

EACH YEAR, I sit down with lists of locomotives from across the model railway sector to work out what has been made, what has been announced and which items are still pending a release date. It's a fascinating process and while exploring the potential of what is coming next, it's easy to be captivated by the future.

Interestingly, this year had seen a reduction in the amount of promised new locomotives by the time we closed for press with the Yearbook, although I'm sure there will be additions to the lists we have here once the Warley National Model Railway Exhibition has taken place in late November.

Why is there apparently less on offer for the future? Three reasons: first, the listings in our 2017 Yearbook were at an exceptional level; secondly we've clearly had a good year for model production with an impressive 21 locomotives being released in 'OO' alone during the year; and thirdly, there haven't been as many announcements as in previous years.

Taking that third point on its own, a reduction in new model projects being announced isn't necessarily a bad thing. A couple of years ago we reached a position where more models were being announced than released, but over the course of 2016 and, in particular 2017, the

Dapol's next 'OO' release is the GWR AEC railcar, due in late 2017.

tables have turned and our manufacturers have been catching up. Hornby has put in a lot of work here to ensure that its models are produced much more closely to its catalogue dates and we now expect that all of its new tooling items for 2017 will be delivered to the retailers before the end of March 2018.

Bachmann has also started to pick up the pace with four new locomotives, as well as carriages and wagons, being released during 2017, but it still has some way to go to catch up on its backlog of promised models. It isn't alone in that though and in the fullness of time all of its projects will be available.

'OO' gauge

Planned models for 'OO' gauge are now at their lowest level since 2015 with 39 on the table. That consists of 15 steam locomotives, down six from 2016, and 24 diesel and electric locomotives and multiple units. »

The 'O' gauge '8750' 0-6-0PT from Dapol is making good progress. This is the first engineering sample.

Gresley's magnificent 'A4' 4-6-2s are never far from the limelight and in 2018 Hatton's is set to release its 'O' gauge model. 4495 *Golden Fleece* passes Stoke signalbox with the up 'West Riding Limited' from Leeds to London King's Cross on June 7 1938. T.G. Hepburn/Rail Archive Stephenson.

Hornby's new Class 87 for 'OO' will cover early and late locomotives including this version as 87035 *Robert Burns* in BR blue.

Class 414 2-HAP third-rail EMU 6095 draws out of the carriage sheds at Dover Marine in September 1972. These two-car units are the subject of one of Bachmann's latest Southern Region multiple units for 'OO'.
Railphotoprints.co.uk.

Left: In 'N' gauge Bachmann is developing this model of the Wainwright 'C' 0-6-0 for its Graham Farish range.

Below: Hatton's has received 3D printed samples from the CAD drawings for its 'O' gauge Gresley 'A3' and 'A4' 4-6-2s.

There is still plenty to look forward to and it is clear that tank engines are currently leading the charge with 75% of the steam outline models being of this nature. That includes Hatton's September announcements of the South Eastern & Chatham Railway (SECR) 'P' 0-6-0T and Andrew Barclay 0-4-0ST as well as models of the LNER 'N7' 0-6-2T from Oxford Rail, the long awaited GWR '94XX' 0-6-0PT from Bachmann and the very soon to be released

SECR 'H' 0-4-4T from Hornby. This is now just around the corner with the first expected in stock during November 2017.

The Southern and Eastern Regions are attracting the greatest attention on the steam front with highlights being the London Brighton and South Coast Railway (LBSCR) 'H2' 4-4-2 from Bachmann along with the aforementioned 'H' and 'P' tank engines.

Moving to more modern motive power, and there is a clear shift towards filling gaps in the electric camp and, impressively, to modelling more multiple units covering diesel as well as electrics. West Coast Main Line (WCML) modellers are set for brand new choices with the Class 87 from Hornby, Class 90 from Bachmann and crowd-funded Class 92 by DJ Models. These three locomotives will make it feasible to accurately model WCML operations in the early 2000s, alongside Heljan's previous model of the Class 86.

The multiple unit fleet is set to grow significantly and following the recent releases of the 4-TC and Class 450 for 'OO' we still have the 2-HAP and 4-BEP to look forward to for the Southern as well as the Class 117, 121, 142 and 158 DMUs. Hornby's model of the Class 800 Intercity Express Programme (IEP) units is currently forecast for release in January 2018.

Kernow's long planned model of the North British prototype 'Warship' diesel-hydraulics is now making good progress with receipt of the first full engineering sample during early October and this is set to be very popular.

Even with fewer announcements, there is still plenty to look forward to - see Table 1.

'N' gauge

The 'N' gauge market hasn't had the strongest year during 2017, whether you look at it from the release or announcement front. However, it is still gaining support from Bachmann and Dapol as well as with crowd-funded models produced through Revolution Trains.

Happily, we have seen key new announcements from the main manufacturers with Bachmann committing to production of the SECR 'C' 0-6-0 and the LMS Stanier '8F' 2-8-0 for steam modellers as well as refurbished versions of the Class 31 as well as a modified version of the Class 70 to model the 70/8 series.

Dapol has also made its return to the 'N' gauge market after putting its projects on hold for assessment earlier in the year. At its annual »

TABLE 1 - 'OO' GAUGE NEW RELEASES FOR – 2018-ONWARDS			
Class	**Region**	**Manufacturer**	**Expected**
GWR steam railmotor	Western	Kernow MRC	TBA
GWR '47XX' 2-8-0	Western	Heljan	2017
GWR '94XX' 0-6-0PT	Western	Bachmann	TBA
LSWR 'B4' 0-4-0T	Southern	Dapol	2018
LBSCR 'H2' 4-4-2T	Southern	Bachmann	2017
SECR 'H' 0-4-4T	Southern	Hornby	2017
SECR 'P' 0-6-0T	Southern	Hatton's	2017/18
GNR Stirling single 4-2-2	Eastern	Rapido Trains/Locomotion	TBA
Midland '1P' 0-4-4T	Midland	Bachmann	TBA
LNER 'J70' 0-6-0VBT	Eastern	Bauer Media	TBA
LNER 'J72' 0-6-0T	Eastern	Bachmann	TBA
LNER 'N7' 0-6-2T	Eastern	Oxford Rail	2018
LNER 'V2' 2-6-2	Eastern	Bachmann	TBA
Andrew Barclay 0-4-0ST	Industrial	Hatton's	2018
Hudswell Clarke 0-6-0ST	Industrial	DJ Models	TBA
AEC GWR railcar	Western	Dapol	2017
Class 07	Southern	Heljan	2017
Class 20/3	Various	Bachmann	TBA
Class 21/29	Scottish	Dapol	TBA
Class 24/1	Various	Bachmann	TBA
Class 24/1	Scottish	Sutton's Loco Works	TBA
Class 41 'Warship'	Western	Kernow MRC	2018
Class 41 prototype HST	Western	Locomotion/Rapido Trains	TBA
Class 59	Western	Dapol	2016
Class 74	Southern	DJ Models	2016
Class 70/8	Various	Bachmann	2017
Class 87	Midland	Hornby	2018
Class 90	Various	Bachmann	TBA
Class 92	Various	DJ Models	TBA
Class 117	Various	Bachmann	TBA
Class 121	Various	Bachmann	TBA
Class 121	Various	Dapol	2017
Class 142	Midland/Eastern	Realtrack	2018
Class 158	Various	Bachmann	2018
Class 410 4-BEP	Southern	Bachmann	TBA
Class 414 2-HAP	Southern	Bachmann	TBA
Class 800	Western/Eastern	Hornby	2018
L&B 2-6-2T ('OO9')	Southern	Heljan	2016
Baldwin 4-6-0T ('OO9')	Industrial	Bachmann	TBA
Total: 39	Steam: 15	Diesel: 24	

open day on October 1 it announced that its 'N' gauge Class 50 project was back on and that it was making a new generation of chassis for the locomotive which will have a Next18 decoder socket as well as a chamber provided for simple conversion to digital sound operation.

Revolution Trains is currently having its Class 390 Pendolino train produced, which has paved the way for it to pursue expressions of interest for a model of the APT-E too – what a model that would be in 'N' gauge! Meanwhile there are still a large number of model projects without a definitive release date for 'N' gauge, but we expect to see many of these gain momentum during 2018.

See Table 2 for the full listing.

'O' gauge

The largest of the three main scales has seen a significant influx of new models and announcements and, interestingly, the commitment from both manufacturer and customers appears equal. Models are being produced, in many cases, in a timely fashion and they are selling through quickly once they are available.

Dapol has been a leading producer of compact locomotives for the scale alongside Minerva Models which has now released three ready-to-run steam engines for 'O'. Heljan continues to champion the main line diesel sector, although it has also begun looking towards multiple units, broadening its appeal »

THE HEADLINES

Planned 'OO' gauge new releases

	2014	2015	2016	2017	2018
Steam:	17	26	25	21	15
Diesel:	13	18	20	25	24
Total:	30	44	45	46	39

Planned 'N' gauge new releases

	2014	2015	2016	2017	2018
Steam:	15	17	13	9	10
Diesel:	15	11	12	14	16
Total:	30	28	25	23	26

Planned 'O' gauge new releases

	2014	2015	2016	2017	2018
Steam:	3	3	3	9	8
Diesel:	9	9	7	11	11
Total:	12	12	10	20	18
Overall total:	72	82	79	87	83

GER 'N7' 0-6-2T 69683 passes Manor Road Sidings with an Enfield Town-Liverpool Street working on April 4 1959. These powerful passenger tanks are to be released in 'OO' gauge by Oxford Rail in 2018. Ken Cook/Rail Archive Stephenson.

Locomotion Models Great Northern Railway 'Single' is expected to become available in 2018. This is the first full engineering sample.

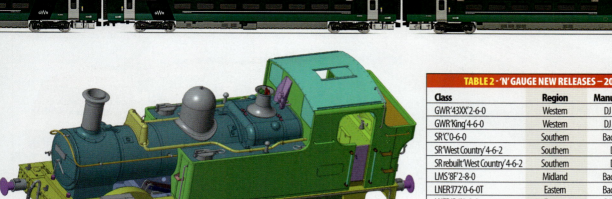

TABLE 2 - 'N' GAUGE NEW RELEASES – 2018-ONWARDS			
Class	**Region**	**Manufacturer**	**Expected**
GWR '43XX' 2-6-0	Western	DJ Models	TBA
GWR 'King' 4-6-0	Western	DJ Models	Proposed
SR 'C' 0-6-0	Southern	Bachmann	2018
SR 'West Country' 4-6-2	Southern	Dapol	TBA
SR rebuilt 'West Country' 4-6-2	Southern	Dapol	TBA
LMS '8F' 2-8-0	Midland	Bachmann	TBA
LNER 'J72' 0-6-0T	Eastern	Bachmann	TBA
LNER 'Q6' 0-8-0	Eastern	DJ Models	TBA
Hunslet 'J94' 0-6-0ST	Eastern	DJ Models	TBA
Hudswell Clarke 0-6-0ST	Industrial	DJ Models	TBA
Hunslet 0-6-0DM	Industrial	N Gauge Society	2018
Class 17	Eastern/Scottish	DJ Models	2018
Class 23	Eastern	DJ Models	TBA
Class 31 (refurbished)	Various	Bachmann	2018
Class 41 prototype HST	Western/Midland	Dapol	2017
Class 50	Midland/Western	Dapol	2018
Class 59	Western	Dapol	TBA
Class 68	Various	Dapol	2018
Class 70/8	Various	Bachmann	2018
Class 92	Various	DJ Models	TBA
Class 92	Various	Revolution Trains	2018
Class 142	Midland/Eastern	Dapol	2018
Class 319	Midland/Southern	Bachmann	TBA
Class 321	Midland/Eastern	Revolution Trains	TBA
Class 390	Midland	Revolution Trains	2017
APT-E	Midland	Revolution Trains	Proposed
Total: 26	Steam: 10	Diesel: 16	

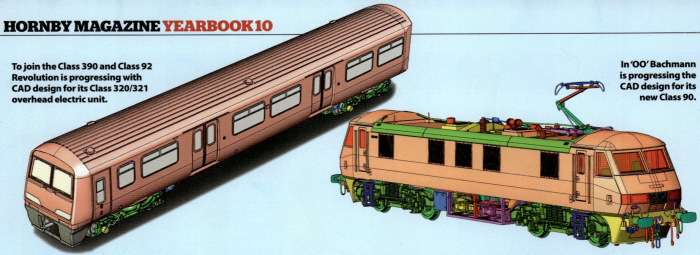

To join the Class 390 and Class 92 Revolution is progressing with CAD design for its Class 320/321 overhead electric unit.

In 'OO' Bachmann is progressing the CAD design for its new Class 90.

and the options available to the modeller.

In 2017 the Little Loco Co debuted its first ready-to-run locomotive in the BTH Class 15 and it is now working on the Ruston 48DS 4wDM shunter which will be produced in England and all versions will be DCC fitted with a sound option available too.

This will be followed by a crowd-funded model of the Class 50 for 'O' gauge by Little Loco, although Heljan has also announced its plan to produce the refurbished version of these popular English Electric Type 4s at the same time.

Interest in steam ready-to-run for 'O' gauge is growing too with Minerva delivering its GWR '8750' 0-6-0PT in late August to be followed by the '57XX' 0-6-0PT before Christmas. Dapol is

working on models of the same GWR 0-6-0PT designs for the scale while it had also just delivered the first of its LMS 'Jinty' 0-6-0Ts as this Yearbook closed for press. Hatton's 'A3' and 'A4' 4-6-2s are on course for release in late 2018 while Heljan is also progressing with delivery of its first steam outline models for the scale covering the GWR '61XX' 2-6-2T and '43XX' 2-6-0.

Table 3 details the full list of planned ready-to-run mass-produced 'O' gauge locomotives.

Overview

With more than 82 new locomotives to look forward to over three scales, even with a lower level of announcements, there is still an impressive list of products to come. From the

compact, like the 'B4' 0-4-0T to the impressive, like the GWR '47XX' 2-8-0: no matter what area or period you model, there is something to entice your wallet in the accompanying tables with this feature.

The rise of 'O' gauge is encouraging and, as you can read on pages 86-91, it isn't confined to locomotives either as there is new support for passenger and freight rolling stock in the scale. 'N' gauge may have taken a back seat for brand new products, but it has still been supported with reliveries of existing products throughout the year and there is plenty on the cards for 2018 and beyond.

As ever, 'OO' gauge is at the heart of the hobby with the most support from manufacturers and customers alike and,

Class 20s are back in vogue for 'O' gauge with Heljan promising the centre headcode version for release in late 2017/early 2018. On May 15 1980 20178 double heads with 20143 through Gloucester working a Bescot-Severn Tunnel Junction mixed freight. Gordon Edgar/Railphotoprints.co.uk.